The Scorpio Book
Everything You Should Know About Scorpios

CRAFTED BY SKRIUWER

Copyright © 2025 by Skriuwer.

All rights reserved. No part of this book may be used or reproduced in any form whatsoever without written permission except in the case of brief quotations in critical articles or reviews.

At **Skriuwer**, we're more than just a team—we're a global community of people who love books. In Frisian, "Skriuwer" means "writer," and that's at the heart of what we do: creating and sharing books with readers worldwide. Wherever you are in the world, **Skriuwer** is here to inspire learning.

Frisian is one of the oldest languages in Europe, closely related to English and Dutch, and is spoken by about **500,000 people** in the province of **Friesland** (Fryslân), located in the northern Netherlands. It's the second official language of the Netherlands, but like many minority languages, Frisian faces the challenge of survival in a modern, globalized world.

We're using the money we earn to promote the Frisian language.

For more information, contact : **kontakt@skriuwer.com** (www.skriuwer.com)

TABLE OF CONTENTS

CHAPTER 1: SCORPIO BASICS

- Dates and basic identity (October 23–November 21)
- Overview of common Scorpio traits
- First impressions and calm intensity

CHAPTER 2: HISTORY OF SCORPIO

- Early Babylonian and Greek roots
- Influences of myth and constellation stories
- Evolution of Scorpio's image through history

CHAPTER 3: SCORPIO'S SYMBOL & ELEMENT

- Scorpion glyph and hidden strength
- Meaning of the water element
- How the symbol and element shape Scorpio's nature

CHAPTER 4: KEY STRENGTHS OF SCORPIO

- Loyalty and steady determination
- Sense of honesty and fairness
- Resourcefulness in problem-solving

CHAPTER 5: KNOWN WEAKNESSES OF SCORPIO

- Holding grudges and suspicion
- Risk of jealousy and need for control
- Managing stubbornness and moodiness

CHAPTER 6: SCORPIO & FEELINGS

- *Deep emotional layers and empathy*
- *Importance of privacy and self-reflection*
- *Healthy ways to handle strong emotions*

CHAPTER 7: SCORPIO AS A FRIEND

- *Observational style in group settings*
- *Forming loyal connections with a few*
- *Maintaining respect and honesty in friendships*

CHAPTER 8: SCORPIO AT HOME

- *Desire for a private, comfortable space*
- *Family interactions and quiet support*
- *Balancing protectiveness with openness*

CHAPTER 9: SCORPIO AT WORK

- *Focus on thoroughness and ethics*
- *Calm leadership and investigative skill*
- *Thriving in roles needing depth and analysis*

CHAPTER 10: SCORPIO & LOVE

- *Intensity and deep commitment*
- *Challenges with jealousy and trust*
- *Building strong bonds through honesty*

CHAPTER 11: SCORPIO & COMMUNICATION

- Observation before speaking
- Direct honesty mixed with privacy
- Reading subtle cues and body language

CHAPTER 12: SCORPIO & DAILY ROUTINES

- Value of structure and introspection
- Scheduling quiet breaks and personal projects
- Balancing discipline with emotional needs

CHAPTER 13: SCORPIO WITH GROUPS

- Group dynamics and cautious participation
- Roles as problem-solvers or calm leaders
- Staying loyal while avoiding power struggles

CHAPTER 14: NOTABLE PEOPLE WITH SCORPIO BIRTHDAYS

- Examples of famous Scorpios in various fields
- Shared traits of determination and depth
- Inspiration drawn from Scorpio achievements

CHAPTER 15: COMMON MYTHS ABOUT SCORPIO

- Exploring misconceptions like secrecy or vengeance
- Why these stereotypes often miss reality
- Balanced view of Scorpio's true character

CHAPTER 16: SCORPIO'S FAVORITE ACTIVITIES

- *Drawn to depth in hobbies, like reading or puzzles*
- *Creative or mindful pursuits for emotional release*
- *Finding meaning in purposeful tasks*

CHAPTER 17: SCORPIO WITH OTHER SIGNS

- *Differences and similarities with each zodiac sign*
- *Where harmony and conflict may arise*
- *Keys to better partnerships or teamwork*

CHAPTER 18: SCORPIO IN DIFFERENT PARTS OF LIFE

- *Childhood curiosity and forming trust*
- *Adulthood challenges in work and family*
- *Reflections in later years and shared wisdom*

CHAPTER 19: TIPS FOR SCORPIO

- *Practical advice for managing strong emotions*
- *Building trust and clear communication*
- *Balancing self-protection with openness*

CHAPTER 20: FINAL THOUGHTS ON SCORPIO

- *Bringing all insights together*
- *Encouraging loyalty, growth, and honest ties*
- *Reflecting on Scorpio's transformative power*

CHAPTER 1: SCORPIO BASICS

Scorpio is the eighth sign of the zodiac. People who are born between October 23 and November 21 are usually called Scorpios. They are often linked to the scorpion symbol, which is a small but strong creature. Many people think Scorpios are mysterious and hard to understand. This is because their feelings can be very deep, and they often keep these feelings hidden from others. Scorpios are said to be brave and determined. They might not always show their true thoughts on the outside, but they often have many ideas on the inside. If you know someone with a birthday in late October or early November, they could be a Scorpio.

Some people say that Scorpio is one of the most intense signs. This means a Scorpio person might feel things very strongly, whether it is happiness, sadness, or excitement. Because they feel things deeply, they might also show a lot of care toward friends and family. But Scorpios can also be quiet, preferring to keep some distance until they feel safe with someone. When they trust another person, they can be very loyal. But when they feel betrayed, they might become distant or upset. It is important to remember that each person is different, so these traits do not apply to everyone all the time.

In astrology, each zodiac sign is linked to an element. Scorpio's element is water. Water signs are often known for strong feelings, creativity, and an interest in understanding the deeper parts of life. The other water signs are Cancer and Pisces. But Scorpio has its own style. It may be seen as the water sign with the most power, because Scorpio is known for its energy and focus. A Scorpio may seem quiet on the outside, yet a lot can be happening in their mind. They might watch carefully before deciding what to do. This calm watching can make them good at guessing what others feel.

Scorpio is also linked to a planet called Pluto, and in older forms of astrology, it is linked to Mars. Pluto is often seen as a planet that represents big changes, secrets, and deep growth. Mars is seen as a planet of action and drive. This pairing gives Scorpio a mix of calm thought and strong passion. When people say Scorpio is ruled by Pluto, they mean Scorpio can focus on things below the surface of life. When people say Scorpio is also connected to Mars, they mean Scorpio can be quick to take action when it is needed. This sign is not afraid of facing challenges.

Many people want to know basic things about Scorpio. For example, they wonder if Scorpios are kind, patient, or thoughtful. Others want to know if Scorpios can be moody or distant. The truth is that each Scorpio can be a bit different. Some are very friendly, while others are more private. Yet, many Scorpios share a wish for truth. They want to find out what is really going on in a situation. They can be very curious about life's mysteries. They might also have strong willpower, which helps them reach their goals. This can make them reliable friends, family members, or teammates.

Scorpios may not always talk about their feelings, but they are often very aware of them. This can make them look serious. Sometimes, they might prefer quiet places over loud, busy ones. That does not mean they do not like having fun. But they may have their own ways of having a good time, such as reading books, watching movies, or thinking about life's big questions. If they trust a person, they might share some secrets. But if they do not feel safe, they may keep their thoughts hidden. This can make Scorpios seem puzzling to those who do not know them well.

Sometimes people think Scorpios are scary or mean. This is not true for everyone. A Scorpio might have a strong presence, so others might feel nervous around them. But many Scorpios can also be caring and loyal. They might remember small details about their loved ones, such as a favorite snack or a special date, and then use that knowledge to show kindness. A Scorpio friend might keep your secrets safe. A Scorpio brother or sister might stand by you in hard times. Their strong focus can also help them to do well in activities they truly care about.

Scorpios often value trust and honesty. If they feel someone is hiding the truth, they might get suspicious. Scorpios like to test their trust in others by asking questions or by watching how people behave over time. They want to see if a person's words match their actions. If a Scorpio finds a true friend, they might stick to that friend for life. But if trust is broken, Scorpios might pull away. This can happen in friendships, families, and teams. Understanding this helps us see that Scorpios take emotional connections very seriously. They do not like to share personal matters with everyone.

Because Scorpio is a water sign, it has some things in common with Cancer and Pisces. All water signs are linked to feelings, imagination, and understanding. Yet each water sign has its own style. Cancer might be more open about feelings, while Pisces might be more dreamy. Scorpio tends to hold feelings close. Scorpios can use their powerful focus in different ways. Some become excellent at solving puzzles, because they can stick with a problem until they find an answer. Others use that focus in creative areas like writing or art. They might enjoy expressing their inner world through pictures or words.

The symbol for Scorpio, the scorpion, can tell us something about this sign. A scorpion is a small creature that can protect itself with a sharp stinger. This might represent how a Scorpio person can stand up for themselves if they feel threatened. But scorpions also try to avoid trouble if they can. Many times, they prefer to hide or move away instead of fighting. Likewise, Scorpios might not show all their strength unless they believe they have to. This hidden power can make them seem intimidating to some people. However, many Scorpios do not like hurting others unless they feel they have no choice.

Some people think Scorpio is a sign of transformation or big changes. This is because Scorpio's ruling planet, Pluto, is often connected to deep changes in life. A Scorpio might go through many shifts in their feelings or beliefs. They could start with one idea and, after thinking deeply, change their mind. They might feel better after they allow themselves to look at their feelings in an honest way. Sometimes, it can be hard to be a Scorpio because the feelings can be so strong. But many Scorpios learn to use these strong feelings to fuel their projects and to help other people.

In a group of friends, you might recognize a Scorpio because they might be the one who listens more than they speak. They often like to observe and figure out who they can trust. Once they feel comfortable, they might open up and become a devoted friend. If you tell them your troubles, they could remember what you said and even offer help later. If you treat them with respect, they often will do the same in return. But if they sense that someone is dishonest or teasing them in a mean way, they could become guarded or even upset.

Scorpios also like to look into many topics. For example, a Scorpio child might enjoy reading books about space, animals, or mysteries. They could spend hours trying to learn everything about a subject they like. When they find a topic that sparks their interest, they might read a lot or practice a lot to get better at it. This might make them very good at school subjects like science or writing. They might also enjoy doing experiments or digging for facts. Their interest in what lies beneath the surface can make them ask many questions. They want to know why and how things happen.

One key idea for understanding Scorpio is depth. A Scorpio often wants to go beyond what is on the outside. This can show up in conversations, where they might not be satisfied with simple answers. They might want to ask more. It can also show up in activities, where they want to learn more details. This search for depth can help them become experts in the fields they care about. But it can also make them more serious than some other signs. They might find simple chats or small talk less interesting, preferring to focus on real connections and honest sharing.

Scorpios can also be very protective of those they love. If you are close to a Scorpio, they might stand up for you. They do not like to see unfairness or wrongdoing toward the people they care about. This protective nature comes from their strong feelings. When they decide that someone matters to them, they will go a long way to help. This loyalty can make Scorpios powerful friends. On the other hand, if they think someone is trying to harm them or their loved ones, they can react with strong anger. They might hold onto a grudge if they feel hurt.

Some Scorpios are drawn to finding answers to difficult questions. They might enjoy activities that allow them to study the hidden sides of life. For instance, they could like detective stories or real-life mysteries. They might be drawn to science experiments, where they can see how things change under different conditions. Or they might be good at tasks that need careful planning. Because of their focus, they can do well in fields such as research, where they are allowed to search for truth. Of course, not every Scorpio will follow the same path. But many share an interest in looking beneath appearances.

Even though Scorpios are often private, this does not mean they do not want friends. They can be friendly in their own way, but they usually pick their friends wisely. They might have fewer close friends compared to some signs, but those friendships can last a long time. If a Scorpio trusts you, they might show you a softer side. They can share their dreams and worries once they feel safe. They might also be good at keeping secrets, so you can tell them something personal without worrying that everyone else will find out. A Scorpio's loyalty is one of their special gifts.

When talking about Scorpio, some people focus on the sign's so-called dark side. They might say Scorpios are too intense, jealous, or suspicious. It is true that Scorpios can become jealous if they believe someone is betraying them. They might also feel suspicious if they think information is being kept from them. But they can learn to handle these feelings in healthy ways. Many Scorpios find ways to manage their strong emotions by expressing them through art, sports, or other activities. Also, not all Scorpios show these traits often. It depends on many factors, like their environment and personal choices.

Another thing to keep in mind is that Scorpios might change over time. They might grow from being a shy person to someone more open, once they have learned to trust. They might also become calmer as they figure out ways to manage their feelings. Some Scorpios could even surprise you by showing a light-hearted side when you least expect it. Their ability to surprise is one reason why people often call Scorpio a complicated sign. But complicated does not have to mean bad. It can mean there is a lot to discover, and there is more than meets the eye.

Scorpios are often seen as leaders in certain situations. Their strong focus helps them stick to tasks. They can handle projects that others find overwhelming. They usually like to finish what they start and do it well. If they are in a group, they might quietly take note of everything. Then, when they have an idea, they offer it. Because they have spent time thinking it through, it can be a good suggestion.

Others might be impressed by their determination. This does not mean all Scorpios want to be leaders, but they often have the traits that can help them lead if they choose.

Many Scorpios have a natural sense of fairness. They can be kind and caring, but they also expect respect in return. They notice when someone acts dishonestly or tries to take advantage of others. They might not always speak up right away, but they will remember it. In a family, a Scorpio child might become upset if they feel a rule is unfair. In a classroom, a Scorpio student might stand up for a friend if they sense something is wrong. This sense of fairness is tied to their strong feelings and their wish to see truth respected.

When thinking about a Scorpio's basic style, it is helpful to picture still water. On the surface, everything looks calm. But below, there is movement and life that you cannot see. Scorpio's strong emotions are like that hidden movement. They do not always show these feelings to the world. If you are patient and treat them kindly, a Scorpio might let you see more of what they really think and feel. If they trust you, they can be warm and caring. If they do not, they might remain guarded. Building trust with a Scorpio can take time, but it can be very rewarding.

Scorpios often think a lot about loyalty. They ask themselves if someone is truly on their side. They might even test a person's loyalty in small ways, such as seeing how that person acts in different situations. This can be puzzling to friends who do not realize they are being tested. But for a Scorpio, loyalty is a big deal. They do not want to share their secrets or form close bonds with people who might break their trust. Once they find someone who is loyal, they may return that loyalty many times over. In this way, Scorpios can form very strong connections.

Scorpio is also linked to the color red, as well as shades of deep purple and black. These colors might remind us of strong feelings or secrets. Some Scorpios like to wear these colors because they feel powerful or confident in them. But not every Scorpio will like the same colors. Still, these colors often show up when talking about Scorpio in astrology. You might see scorpion symbols in red or purple in books and magazines. This is one more way people connect Scorpio with mystery and power. The depth and intensity of these colors match what many see as Scorpio's inner strength.

Some say that Scorpio is like the detective of the zodiac. This is because of Scorpio's keen sense of observation. A Scorpio may notice small changes in someone's voice or behavior. They might see clues that others miss. This trait can help them discover the truth in many situations. It can also make them good at understanding what motivates people. They might guess how someone feels before that person even says it. Of course, not every Scorpio is the same, but many share this talent for careful watching and piecing together information. It is one of the reasons they seem so mysterious.

Another feature of Scorpio is strong determination. When they decide they want something, they will work very hard to achieve it. If it seems hard or takes a long time, they might keep going anyway. This can be an advantage in school, sports, or creative tasks. Their focus helps them learn new skills and keep practicing. Sometimes, they do not give up even when others tell them the goal might be out of reach. They believe that if they use their energy in the right way, they can reach the result they want. This sense of purpose can be inspiring to others.

Because Scorpio is tied to water, some Scorpios find calmness in water activities. This could include swimming, fishing, or simply enjoying the sound of waves. Water might feel relaxing to them, allowing them to let go of tension. Of course, this is not true for every Scorpio, but many do feel a connection to water. They might also like listening to rain or sitting near a pond. Water can help them find balance, since water is their ruling element. It can soothe their intense feelings and give them space to think. Spending quiet time in a calm place can make a Scorpio feel at ease.

When it comes to hobbies, Scorpios might pick activities that let them use their detective-like minds. They could enjoy puzzles, riddles, or escape rooms. They might also like strategy games where they can plan moves carefully. Some may enjoy reading mystery books or watching mystery shows. Others might prefer to write their own stories or create art that shows how they feel inside. Because they have strong focus, they can excel at many tasks if they decide it is worth their time. They may also practice until they master something, which can lead them to become very good at what they do.

Scorpio children can be loving, but they might need a bit of privacy. They often enjoy having a special place to think. They might not talk about their thoughts right away, even with family members. If they have parents or guardians who respect their need for quiet time, they may feel more comfortable sharing later. Scorpio children might also show a strong will if they believe something is important. It can be helpful for the adults in their life to talk with them gently about why certain rules exist. Once they understand the reasons, they might be more willing to cooperate.

A Scorpio may have a special interest in understanding people's motives. They like to know what drives a person to do something. This can lead them to become good listeners, even if they do not talk much themselves. They might hear a friend's problem and offer a few careful words of advice. Or they might wait, gather information, and speak up only when they have a clear picture. This quiet listening can make them good friends and family members. They are often able to pick up on things others miss, like a subtle change in a person's mood or a small clue in a situation.

Scorpios can also be very creative. Their deep feelings might push them to paint, write, sing, or dance. They often want to express the things they feel inside, but it can be hard for them to talk about these feelings with words. Through art, music, or other outlets, they can share parts of themselves. A Scorpio who loves drawing might use dark or vibrant colors. A Scorpio who writes stories might enjoy creating characters who have strong emotions. Because Scorpio is associated with depth, many find that creative activities are a good way to channel their energy in a positive manner.

Some people wonder if Scorpios are always serious. While many Scorpios do have a serious side, they can also be funny or playful. Their sense of humor might be a little different, sometimes wry or sarcastic, but it can be entertaining. They might tease friends or family in a lighthearted way if they feel comfortable. However, they usually show this lighter side only after they trust the people around them. At first, they might appear quiet or reserved. Over time, as they feel more at ease, they may reveal a warm, caring, and even silly nature that surprises those who do not know them well.

Because Scorpio is connected with powerful emotions, Scorpios can sometimes feel overwhelmed if they do not find healthy ways to handle stress. They might hold onto worries or hurt feelings. It can help them to talk with someone they trust, but they might need extra time to feel safe doing so. Activities like writing in a journal or exercising can help them let go of tension. Some might turn to music or painting. Others might prefer spending time outdoors in nature. Finding a healthy way to handle their emotions is important for Scorpios, because holding everything inside can make them feel heavy or tired.

The Scorpio sign is also linked to confidence. When a Scorpio believes in themselves, they can do great things. Their intense focus and strong will can help them stand out in many fields, like science,

art, writing, or even helping people. They can speak up for what they believe is right. But if a Scorpio loses confidence, they might become quite self-critical. They might question themselves a lot and wonder if they are good enough. Finding balance and trusting their strengths is important. With support from friends and family, Scorpios can learn to see the good in themselves and in others around them.

Scorpios often look for real connections. They are not usually interested in false flattery or shallow relationships. They want the truth, even if it is hard to hear. Because of this, they might prefer one close friend over many casual acquaintances. They can be suspicious of people who seem fake. If someone tries to pretend they are something they are not, a Scorpio can often sense it. They appreciate honesty more than anything. This can sometimes lead to conflicts if others are not comfortable with directness. But Scorpios feel that honest communication is the best way to build strong bonds with people.

When it comes to group settings, a Scorpio might not always jump in right away. They could stand to the side, quietly studying the group. Then, after they have a good sense of who is friendly or trustworthy, they might join the conversation. This can make them appear reserved. But inside, they might be assessing every detail. Once they start speaking, people might notice how thoughtful or direct they can be. They usually do not say things just to please others; they speak what they really think. This approach can earn them respect, though it can also lead to disagreements if others prefer polite but less honest chats.

Scorpios can be drawn to subjects like science, psychology, mysteries, or even space. These areas allow them to look for answers and see beyond the surface. They might like reading about black holes, ancient civilizations, or the inner workings of the mind. These topics match their desire to uncover secrets or truths. A Scorpio may also enjoy tasks that let them research or experiment. If they have access to a library, a computer, or a set of tools, they can spend hours learning. This can be exciting for them because it fits their natural drive to discover what is hidden.

One thing to remember is that Scorpio's way of thinking can be very focused. This focus can be a gift, helping them become really good at what they choose to study. But it can also be a challenge if they get stuck thinking about negative things. They might dwell on a problem for a long time, feeling upset or worried. It can help them to take breaks and do things that make them feel calm. For example, talking to a kind friend or playing a sport. If they find healthy ways to handle heavy thoughts, they can keep their mind clear and energetic.

Many Scorpios have a strong moral compass. They believe in doing what they see as right. Sometimes, they might clash with people who do not share these beliefs. Scorpios can feel very passionate about what they consider good or fair. If they witness something they think is wrong, they might speak out or try to fix it. They can be brave in standing up against problems. Some Scorpios might choose jobs or roles where they can fight for fairness. Others might help their friends and family by offering support when someone is treated badly. Their strength of purpose can be a big part of who they are.

Even though Scorpios can seem strong on the outside, they also need kindness and support. Sometimes, people believe that because Scorpios can be tough, they do not need anyone's help. But like everyone else, Scorpios want understanding and care. They might not always ask for help, but a gentle question like, "How are you feeling?" can mean a lot. If a Scorpio trusts you, they might open up and share their worries. They may appreciate someone who listens without judging. Their hard shell is there to protect their soft inside.

If you earn their trust, you might see a sensitive heart hidden underneath.

Scorpio's nature can also be seen in their relationships with pets or animals. Some Scorpios have a gentle spot for animals in need. They might quietly help a stray cat or volunteer to take care of a neighbor's dog. Because of their deep feelings, they can connect strongly with animals that rely on kindness. They might also be very good at understanding an animal's mood or need for space. This caring side shows that Scorpios are not just about power and intensity; they also have empathy for living beings. This can make them good pet owners or volunteers at animal shelters.

People sometimes misunderstand Scorpios because of the sign's reputation. They might think of Scorpios as always vengeful or mean. While some Scorpios can hold grudges, many learn to manage these feelings by understanding that holding onto anger can hurt them too. They can grow and change just like anyone else. With time and wisdom, a Scorpio can let go of past hurts and move toward better connections. This sign's depth can help them learn from experiences in a strong way. They can reflect on what happened and figure out how to avoid problems in the future. In this sense, Scorpio can transform negativity into growth.

Scorpio is sometimes said to be a sign of extremes. A Scorpio might see things in strong colors, like black and white, instead of gray. They might love something or hate it, trust someone or not trust them at all. With patience and understanding, they can learn to see the middle ground. This can help them be more flexible. But their strong nature also has advantages, because they do not do things halfway. They put their heart into what they care about. That can lead to great success if they aim their determination at good goals. It can also bring strong feelings of pride when they accomplish something hard.

Scorpios are often drawn to honesty, depth, and loyalty. These basics about Scorpio can help you understand why they do what they do. They are not always simple to figure out, but that adds to their charm. A Scorpio child or adult might test your patience, but they can also offer great friendship. They will remember kind acts for a long time, just as they might remember hurts. If you have a Scorpio in your life, knowing these traits may help you connect with them better. You might learn to be patient, honest, and respectful, and in return, you could earn a friend or family member who stands by you.

In summary, Scorpio's basics involve depth, strong feelings, and a quiet determination. This sign can be both gentle and fierce. Understanding these qualities is the first step to appreciating the Scorpio way. Although they can be secretive, Scorpios have a big capacity for love and devotion. They might not share every thought they have, but when they do, they mean it. Scorpios can bring passion and loyalty to any area of life they care about. They protect what they treasure, and they can show great kindness to those who earn their trust. This chapter gives an overview of Scorpio's main traits, setting the stage for deeper learning.

CHAPTER 2: HISTORY OF SCORPIO

Astrology, which is the study of the zodiac signs, has been around for thousands of years. To understand how Scorpio got its name and meaning, it helps to look at history. In many ancient cultures, people looked at the stars and made shapes called constellations. One of these constellations was called Scorpius, which looked like a scorpion in the sky. Over time, this constellation gave rise to the zodiac sign Scorpio. The scorpion shape in the sky helped people remember the traits linked to this sign. Different cultures had different stories about the scorpion, but many of them saw it as a creature of power and mystery.

The Babylonian people, who lived in the region of Mesopotamia, were among the first to group stars into zodiac constellations. Their ancient records show that they recognized a scorpion-like shape in the sky. Later, the ancient Greeks took these star groups and built myths around them. In Greek mythology, the scorpion was sometimes connected to the story of Orion, a hunter who was said to have been fatally stung by a giant scorpion sent by the earth goddess. This story linked the scorpion to themes of danger and hidden strength. Over time, the constellation's name and shape were passed on, becoming Scorpio in Latin.

Egyptian astrology also had ideas about the scorpion. In some tales, the scorpion was linked to the goddess Isis, who used scorpions to protect her. This connection of the scorpion with both protection and harm shows up in many stories. On one hand, the scorpion's sting could be dangerous. On the other hand, the scorpion could defend against enemies. As people traveled and traded information, these stories mixed and changed. But the idea of the scorpion as a symbol of mystery, defense, and powerful emotion stayed. This laid the groundwork for how Scorpio would later be seen in Western astrology.

When the Romans adopted many of the Greek gods and myths, they also kept the zodiac constellations. They Latinized the names, so Scorpius became Scorpio. They used astrology for various purposes, such as predicting events or trying to understand a person's character. Even some rulers looked to astrology for guidance. While not everyone agreed with these beliefs, astrology still spread and became a common point of reference in many cultures. By the time of the Middle Ages in Europe, Scorpio was firmly recognized as the eighth zodiac sign, and it was linked to ideas of transformation, hidden power, and strong will.

In ancient times, the zodiac signs were also linked to the seasons. Scorpio season falls in late autumn in the Northern Hemisphere, a time when the weather grows colder and leaves change color. This part of the year can feel a bit mysterious, with shorter days and longer nights. People in olden days often linked these changes to Scorpio's themes of going within, being secretive, and dealing with darker or deeper thoughts. Harvest festivals or other seasonal events often took place around this time, and though beliefs varied, many saw this period as a moment for reflection on life's changes and endings.

Because Scorpio is connected to transformation, ancient astrologers wrote that people born under this sign might experience major shifts in their lives. This idea came from the link to the scorpion, which can hide in dark places and then emerge suddenly. Old texts mention that Scorpio's energy can be intense and that it pushes a person to face challenges. In some regions, Scorpio was even considered to have healing qualities, because scorpion venom, in small amounts, could be used as medicine. The dual idea of poison and cure helped shape the complex view of Scorpio as both harmful and helpful, depending on how its power was used.

During the Renaissance, a time of renewed interest in art and science in Europe, astrology continued to evolve. People like Galileo focused on studying the stars with telescopes, but many still kept an interest in astrological ideas. Paintings and illustrations from this time often showed the scorpion as a symbol for Scorpio. Alchemists, who attempted to turn base metals into gold, also used scorpion images in their texts. They believed in processes of breaking things down and building them back up, which matched Scorpio's link to big changes. Although modern science developed, astrology remained popular among certain groups.

In Hindu astrology, known as Vedic astrology, Scorpio is also recognized but called Vrishchika. It shares some traits with Western Scorpio, such as intensity and a connection to deep emotions. However, there are differences in how Vedic astrology calculates dates and interprets planetary positions. Still, the idea of a scorpion as a symbol remains strong. Ancient Sanskrit texts describe the nature of Vrishchika, sometimes emphasizing how this sign can be determined and passionate. The fact that similar traits appear in different parts of the world shows how strongly the image of the scorpion affects people's imaginations, no matter the culture.

Over time, Scorpio came to be ruled by two planets in Western astrology. The first was Mars, the planet of action and aggression, which was the main ruler before Pluto was discovered in 1930. Mars gave Scorpio traits like drive, courage, and sometimes anger. After Pluto was identified, astrologers assigned this distant planet to Scorpio. Pluto is linked to major changes, secrets, and hidden truths. This shift highlighted Scorpio's powerful capacity for renewal. Thus, in more modern forms of astrology, Scorpio has two rulers: Mars (the old ruler) and Pluto (the modern ruler). This dual rulership supports the idea that Scorpio is both fiery and mysterious.

Pluto is a small planet, but astrologers believed its effect was large. Because it sits far from the Sun, it moves slowly, and so it was thought to govern deep, long-lasting changes. When Pluto joined Mars as Scorpio's ruler, the sign's link to secrecy and renewal became stronger in astrological ideas. People said that Scorpio could die and be reborn in some symbolic sense, meaning they could face big problems and come out stronger. This is why some older writings about Scorpio mention a phoenix, a mythical bird that rises from its own ashes. This extra symbol points to Scorpio's theme of growth through trials.

In many older cultures, scorpions were seen as both dangerous and protective. For example, in some parts of Africa and the Middle East, scorpions were respected because their stings could be deadly. People learned to watch for them in the desert or in dark places. Because of this, the scorpion became linked to caution, secrecy, and survival. These ideas were passed into astrology, where Scorpio was known to be watchful and careful. If you think about a scorpion's ability to hide under rocks and only strike when needed, you can see how people might connect this to a person's traits when they are born under Scorpio.

In old Chinese astrology, the concept of a scorpion does not match directly with the Western zodiac. However, there are star groups that somewhat overlap with Scorpius. Ancient Chinese sky maps had a different way of dividing the stars. Still, in modern times, Chinese and Western zodiac ideas sometimes blend, leading people born in certain years to combine their Chinese zodiac animal with their Western sign. For instance, someone might say they are a Scorpio-Rat or a Scorpio-Dragon. These mixes show how people like to gather ideas from different systems, even though each system has its own unique background and rules.

In the Americas, various indigenous cultures also looked at the stars. Some recognized shapes similar to the scorpion, though the stories might have been different. Astronomy was important for tracking seasons, planting, and navigation. Even if the same sign names were not used, the knowledge of star patterns was well developed. The scorpion shape in the sky is quite noticeable if you know where to look. As explorers from Europe visited the Americas, they shared their astrological system, and the concept of Scorpio spread. Over time, Western astrology became more common, though many traditional star stories remain important in local cultures.

The printing press, invented in the 15th century, helped spread astrological information far and wide. Books about astrology became more common, including those that detailed the traits of Scorpio. People who could read had access to these ideas in a way that was not possible before. Almanacs, which listed moon phases and planetary positions, were popular among farmers and city folk alike. Many of these almanacs included sections about each zodiac sign. Scorpio was described as a sign of deep feelings, powerful determination, and hidden strength. As literacy grew, so did the reach of astrological concepts, allowing Scorpio's reputation to become well known.

During the Enlightenment in Europe, some thinkers questioned astrology because it was not based on the scientific method. Yet, people continued to read horoscopes and found them entertaining or helpful. In newspapers and magazines, simple horoscopes became popular in the 20th century. Scorpio's section often mentioned subjects like strong will or secretiveness. Although these short horoscopes did not cover all the depth of astrology, they did shape how the general public saw Scorpio. The sign was talked about as mysterious, passionate, and sometimes jealous. Even though real astrology involves more than just a sun sign, these quick tidbits kept Scorpio in the public mind.

In modern times, books and websites about astrology often mention Scorpio as one of the most misunderstood signs. Historical descriptions paint Scorpio as both a powerful force and a secretive presence. Because of that, many modern astrologers try to show that Scorpio is not just about sting or harm. They discuss Scorpio's capacity for healing, loyalty, and strong friendships. This updated view comes from looking back at the old myths and adjusting them to our current understanding of personal growth and emotional complexity. Scorpio is still considered intense, but it is now also appreciated for its ability to care deeply and stand firm.

Some modern astrologers use three animals to show Scorpio's growth. The first is the scorpion itself, which hides and can strike. The second is the eagle, which soars high and sees the bigger picture, showing Scorpio's ability to rise above problems. The third is the phoenix, which is reborn from ashes, reflecting Scorpio's knack for renewal. These symbols did not come from ancient times in exactly this order but developed over centuries of thought on how Scorpio evolves. Whether one likes this concept or not, it remains a popular way to explain Scorpio's many layers, linking them to stories of growth through challenges.

Across history, Scorpio was often connected with subjects that people found a bit scary or taboo. For instance, in some old texts, Scorpio was linked to secrets, magic, and the unknown. Because the scorpion lives in hidden places and comes out at night, it made sense to ancient people that this sign would rule parts of life that are not always talked about openly. Some connected Scorpio with the afterlife or with hidden knowledge. Even in modern times, people who follow astrology might see Scorpio as a sign that can handle topics others find uncomfortable. This comes from a long legacy of myth and symbolism.

As explorers traveled and continents connected through trade, the scorpion became known in areas where it might not have been common before. This helped the Scorpio symbol spread even more. In regions where scorpions were not local, people learned about them from travelers' stories, sometimes adding new layers to the myth. People might have been told stories of scorpions in deserts or jungles, which made the creature seem exotic and dangerous. This extra sense of mystery may have made Scorpio even more interesting to those studying astrology. They saw the scorpion as an unusual creature that was hard to predict, much like the sign itself.

In some Middle Eastern and African cultures, the scorpion was used in folk medicine. Healers knew how to treat scorpion stings, and some believed certain parts of the scorpion had healing properties. This dual nature—a creature that can harm yet also be used for cures—was not lost on old astrologers. They saw it as a sign that Scorpio could bring both risk and relief. Over time, this idea blended with the sign's meaning. In reading about Scorpio, you might find references to scorpion venom as both a threat and a possible remedy. This goes hand in hand with Scorpio's link to big changes and power.

One reason Scorpio has remained prominent in astrology is that it resonates with universal human themes. Across the centuries, people have faced fear, secrets, and moments of deep feeling. The scorpion serves as a reminder that even small things can hold surprising power. It also points to the idea that facing your fears can lead to strength. This aligns with the stories told by many cultures about scorpions and, by extension, the Scorpio sign. So, Scorpio's history is not just about myths or star positions; it is also about core human emotions like bravery, caution, loyalty, and transformation.

We can also note how Scorpio's historical image shaped the way people see those born under this sign. Ancient beliefs can leave lasting impressions. For example, if a culture taught that scorpions are sneaky, people might assume a Scorpio person is sneaky. But as our knowledge grows, we understand that a Scorpio can be honest and caring too. History provides the roots of these ideas, but modern astrology tries to show the balance. Studying the past helps us see how Scorpio got labeled as mysterious and passionate, while also remembering that not all Scorpios are the same. Each person has their own mix of traits.

As astrology moved into the 21st century, Scorpio kept its place as the sign of depth and feeling. Online communities share memes and jokes about Scorpio being intense or secretive. This modern humor is a new form of storytelling. It continues the tradition of linking the scorpion to certain personality traits. In social media groups, you can find many discussions where people talk about their "Scorpio side" and whether it matches historical descriptions. While some do this just for fun, others take it more seriously. Either way, the history of Scorpio continues to shape how people think about the sign in today's world.

In many languages, Scorpio is recognized by a similar name. The sign's symbol, often written as an "M" with a tail pointing upward, is a key icon in modern astrology charts. This symbol came from medieval scribes who tried to find a simple way to represent the sign's name and nature. Over centuries, this symbol gained acceptance. You can see it on websites, in books, and on jewelry. Sometimes, Scorpios choose to wear their zodiac symbol to show pride in their sign. This continues an old human habit: marking ourselves with symbols that speak to our traits or stories.

If you look at an old star map, you can see that the constellation Scorpius is near the center of the Milky Way in the sky. Ancient observers likely found it fascinating to see such a bright region of stars. They might have imagined the scorpion prowling through the heavens. Many star myths place Orion on one side of the sky and Scorpius on the other, so that when one rises, the other sets. This was seen as a sign that the scorpion and the hunter were forever connected by their myth. Even if science has given us new explanations about stars, the story remains a part of cultural history.

Through each period—Babylonian, Egyptian, Greek, Roman, and beyond—the scorpion image stayed, carrying ideas of power, secret strength, and transformation. Over time, these qualities grew into the modern image of Scorpio. Whether through myths of a giant scorpion that stung Orion or through Egyptian tales of protection, the scorpion always had a special place in stories. People saw it as both harmful and healing, both hidden and fierce. This gave Scorpio a unique position in astrology, different from the other signs. Today, when we talk about Scorpio, we are repeating ideas that have been shaped by thousands of years of human storytelling.

In medieval Europe, scholars who read Latin texts often wrote about the scorpion in bestiaries (books about animals). They noted that while scorpions were small, their stings were painful. This idea of small but mighty stuck with the Scorpio sign. Astrologers connected it to the human ability to hide great power behind a calm exterior. Because the Middle Ages were full of superstition, the scorpion also took on a mystical air. People thought if you saw a scorpion in a dream, it might mean betrayal or hidden danger. Such beliefs carried into astrological writings, shaping Scorpio's reputation for hidden motives and strong reactions.

Over the past century, astrology has gone through periods of widespread popularity, especially in the West. Magazines and newspapers often described Scorpio as a sign that is passionate, mysterious, and sometimes jealous or vengeful. These short pieces trace back to the sign's older images of the scorpion's sting and secretiveness. But more detailed astrological books and teachers pointed out that Scorpio can also be healing, protective, and wise. They reminded readers that the scorpion is not always on the attack. It is often patient, waiting, and only uses its sting to defend itself. This balanced view has become more common in modern times.

Some historians also connect Scorpio's presence in ancient myths to the fact that scorpions appeared in stories worldwide. For instance, the Maya of Central America had their own scorpion myths, and the ancient Chinese had scorpion-like figures in art. While these may not match Western astrology exactly, they show that humans everywhere found scorpions interesting and a bit frightening. Because scorpions can survive in harsh conditions, they became symbols of endurance. This trait can be seen in the Scorpio sign as well. Many Scorpio individuals are said to endure hardships and still stand strong, much like a scorpion that lives in a tough environment.

In the late 19th and early 20th centuries, groups that studied mystic and spiritual topics—such as the Theosophical Society—began to combine astrology with ideas from Eastern religions and other esoteric traditions. Scorpio became connected not just with hidden powers but also with personal growth. Some writings from that era describe Scorpio as a sign that faces darkness inside oneself and turns it into light. While not everyone agrees with this view, it added another layer to Scorpio's story. Many of these ideas are still shared in certain astrological circles, mixing ancient myths with more recent spiritual concepts.

Another shift in Scorpio's historical image came when science advanced and people learned more about scorpions themselves. We discovered that different scorpion species have different levels of venom, and not all are harmful to humans. This paralleled a softer look at Scorpio in astrology. Rather than focusing only on danger, astrologers started to speak about choice and free will. A Scorpio person could use their strong will for good or for bad. They could sting or they could protect. The sign's old reputation for danger remained, but now it was balanced with the idea that a Scorpio can also bring healing and support.

Modern technology, such as powerful telescopes and space probes, has given us more insight into Pluto. While Pluto is no longer classified as a main planet by astronomers, many astrologers still treat it as important. They argue that Pluto's symbolic meaning does not vanish just because of the new classification. Instead, they say Pluto's distant, shadowy nature fits well with Scorpio's history of being tied to secrets and big changes. This viewpoint shows how astrology and astronomy can move along different paths. Science might see Pluto one way, while astrology sees it as a key piece of Scorpio's identity.

In the 1960s and 1970s, there was a surge of interest in astrology, partly tied to counterculture movements. People seeking alternative ways to understand themselves looked to the zodiac. Scorpio's deep image spoke to those who wanted to uncover hidden truths. They felt that Scorpio's willingness to face the darker side of life was refreshing in a society that sometimes avoided discussing such matters. Books published during that time often praised Scorpio for being fearless, while also cautioning about negative traits like jealousy. This renewed focus kept Scorpio in the spotlight, reinforcing its centuries-old reputation as the sign of intensity and hidden strength.

When we read about Scorpio in a historical context, we see a story of a sign that has evolved while keeping its core ideas. The scorpion symbol, from ancient Mesopotamia to Greek myth, from Egyptian lore to Roman astrology, gave birth to Scorpio's place in the zodiac. Over thousands of years, astrologers, myth-makers, and everyday people added their own thoughts and experiences to shape Scorpio's meaning. That meaning includes power, secrecy, emotion, and the ability to change. Each culture added new details to the tale, but the heart of Scorpio remained. That heart is the scorpion's image and the awe it inspires.

Even today, if you look up at the sky during the right time of year, you can see the constellation Scorpius. It has a bright red star named Antares, which is sometimes called the heart of the scorpion. For ancient sky-watchers, that red star might have symbolized the scorpion's sting or its fiery spirit. Modern astronomers study Antares to learn about star life cycles, while astrologers might see it as a star that adds extra intensity to Scorpio. Either way, this bright star has captured human interest for millennia, linking the scorpion in the sky to the zodiac sign we talk about now.

Throughout the long history of Scorpio, one message stands out: there is more to this sign than meets the eye. The scorpion's size might fool you into thinking it is not a threat. But if you are not careful, it can sting. At the same time, it is not always out to harm. Ancient peoples recognized that scorpions have a place in nature's balance, controlling pests and representing a kind of delicate equilibrium. Astrology took this idea further, suggesting that Scorpio's power can be used in many ways. History shows us that those who wrote about Scorpio were both drawn to and wary of its energy.

Mythology also gave Scorpio a place in the sky so that people could remember its tales every time they looked up. Many constellations have stories of heroes or creatures that overcame or caused trouble. The scorpion's story was one of conflict with Orion, teaching lessons about pride, respect, and the might of nature. Over centuries, that story blended with cultural views about scorpions. The sign of Scorpio carried forward these lessons, warning about underestimating something small yet strong. Today, we still find it meaningful, whether through star-gazing, reading astrology texts, or thinking about Scorpio friends who display strong will and passion.

The scorpion also had a place in artworks. In medieval paintings, you might see small scorpion images in the corners, signifying hidden danger. In Renaissance art, scorpions sometimes showed up in allegorical scenes about temptation or knowledge. Later, as printing became cheaper, zodiac images became more stylized. The scorpion might be depicted in a simple line drawing or even turned into a cartoon. But the essence remained: a creature that can defend itself, living in shadowy places, symbolizing both threat and protection. These artistic depictions helped keep Scorpio in the cultural memory, attaching feelings of curiosity, caution, and respect to the sign.

In places where scorpions are common, like deserts or tropical areas, people developed folk stories or sayings that included scorpions. Some might have been warnings, like telling children not to lift rocks in certain places. Others might have been tales of courage, describing someone who managed to catch a scorpion without being stung. Such stories reinforced the idea of scorpions as creatures you do not want to anger. Over time, these attitudes fed into the astrological idea that Scorpio people might react strongly if mistreated. The sign's reputation for a quick sting if harmed made sense to those who saw real scorpions in their daily life.

As we reach modern times, we see that Scorpio's historical evolution is full of depth. Its roots in ancient star lore, myths about gods and heroes, and cultural views on scorpions all shaped its meaning. People who study astrology today still look back at these old stories to understand the sign's foundation. They note how Scorpio went from being just a constellation in the sky to a sign of deep emotion, secrecy, and strength. By looking at these historical threads, we can appreciate why Scorpio stands out among the zodiac signs. It carries a legacy that speaks to human fascination with the hidden and the powerful.

Today, you might read a simple newspaper horoscope for Scorpio that mentions strong feelings or secrecy. But behind those few words is a long history. It includes ancient Babylonian stargazing, Greek myths, Roman naming, medieval superstitions, and modern insights. This mixture of old and new has kept Scorpio relevant for centuries. People continue to find something captivating about the scorpion's image and the themes it represents. While we may no longer believe all the old tales, we still hold onto the sign's core qualities. Scorpio remains a symbol of strong will, hidden depth, and the power to face life's big questions with courage.

Looking at Scorpio through the lens of history reminds us that astrology is not just about daily predictions. It is a system shaped by countless generations of storytellers, observers, and thinkers. Scorpio, in particular, carries many stories about fear, bravery, loyalty, and rebirth. Whether you see these as literal truths or as metaphors, they offer a glimpse into how humans have tried to explain the mysteries of life. In that sense, understanding Scorpio's past can help us see why people still connect with this sign. It gives them a framework for discussing deep feelings and changes, topics that have always been part of human experience.

Over thousands of years, the scorpion in the sky has stayed, shining as a reminder of the scorpion's place in myth. While science has changed how we view the stars, the stories we tell about Scorpio still hold emotional weight. They speak of silent power and hidden dangers, but also of strength and bravery. From ancient temples to modern websites, from stone carvings to digital apps, Scorpio's symbol endures. We can see it as a link between the past and the present, showing how certain ideas remain important to us. Scorpio may have started as a shape in the night sky, but it grew into much more.

In some ways, the history of Scorpio is also a history of astrology itself. Both have faced changes and challenges. Both have been praised, questioned, and revised through the ages. Yet both remain intriguing to many people. Scorpio's story, tied to the scorpion's image, touches on primal concerns of protection, harm, loyalty, and strong emotion. That might be why it has never faded away. Even if someone does not fully believe in astrology, they might still be drawn to the scorpion's drama. They might still find meaning in the story of Orion and the scorpion, or in the idea of Pluto's hidden realm representing unseen truths.

As we close this historical look at Scorpio, remember that each era contributed something to the sign's identity. From the earliest Babylonian star watchers to modern astrologers, people have tried to describe the power they sensed in Scorpio. They gave it myths, symbols, and planetary rulers, all to capture what they felt was special about it. Today, when we say Scorpio is intense, we are echoing voices from thousands of years ago who saw the same traits in the scorpion. By knowing these roots, we can better understand why Scorpio holds such a strong place in astrology and in the hearts of those who are

CHAPTER 3: SCORPIO'S SYMBOL & ELEMENT

Scorpio's official zodiac symbol is the scorpion. This small creature has a curved tail with a stinger at the end, which many people find both fascinating and a bit scary. In astrology, a symbol like this often reflects traits that belong to the sign. For Scorpio, the scorpion can represent hidden power and the ability to react quickly when needed. While some might only think about the sting, the scorpion also stands for being careful and staying alert to threats. This makes sense for Scorpio, a sign known for noticing what others might overlook and for protecting what is important.

When you see pictures of the zodiac signs, Scorpio is usually shown with an "M"-shaped glyph that has a small arrow or hook at the end. This glyph has been used by astrologers to mark Scorpio in charts and books. Some say the "M" could stand for many ancient words, though these ideas vary from source to source. The arrow or tail points outward, hinting at the scorpion's stinger. The overall shape is simple, yet it reminds us of Scorpio's focus. Although modern astrology does not always explain each detail of the glyph, most people can recognize Scorpio right away because of it.

Aside from the scorpion, some astrologers talk about other animals linked to Scorpio, such as the eagle or the phoenix. Even so, the scorpion remains the most common symbol in most writings and art. The eagle and phoenix ideas highlight a higher or more renewed form of Scorpio, but they are not as widespread in everyday discussions. The scorpion shape is easy to draw, and it reminds people of Scorpio's main traits: watchfulness, a sense of caution, and an inner reserve of power. Because of this, the scorpion is the best-known symbol when someone mentions Scorpio among the zodiac signs.

Scorpions in the wild can be found in deserts or other places where they often hide during the day and come out at night. In a similar way, Scorpio folks might enjoy having quiet or private time before they reveal their thoughts or feelings. The scorpion hunts carefully, using its senses to find food. Likewise, a Scorpio person might observe situations closely before acting. This careful approach can give them an advantage, since they are not likely to rush. The scorpion's hard shell also represents Scorpio's ability to protect their heart. They often show a calm surface even when they feel deep emotions inside.

Because the scorpion is known for its sting, many assume Scorpio individuals are always ready to fight. However, real scorpions prefer to avoid fights if they can. They only use their sting when they feel threatened. This detail can help us see that Scorpios do not seek conflict for no reason. They can be direct or strong-willed, but that does not mean they want to harm people. In fact, many Scorpios use their intense energy to reach personal or shared goals. The scorpion symbol shows us the possibility of defense, but it also reminds us that Scorpios, like scorpions, usually wait and watch first.

Apart from the scorpion symbol, Scorpio is also a water sign. In astrology, each sign belongs to one of four elements: Fire, Earth, Air, or Water. Water signs—Cancer, Scorpio, and Pisces—are known for strong emotions, empathy, and intuition. Because Scorpio is a water sign, it holds traits like insight, depth of feeling, and a sense of understanding that goes beyond what is seen on the surface. Water can change shape and flow around obstacles, just as Scorpio can adapt to different situations by tuning into the deeper factors that others might miss. This flexible nature can be a big strength for Scorpio.

Scorpio is the second water sign in the zodiac cycle, with Cancer being the first and Pisces being the third. Some people say Scorpio is like the more intense phase of water. Cancer is often linked to caring and protecting loved ones, while Pisces is often linked to dreams and imagination. Scorpio stands out because it combines emotional sensitivity with focus and resolve. Water can be calm on the surface while holding strong currents beneath. Scorpio's brand of water can be still at first glance, but it has the power to transform and direct its energy in a very determined way.

Because Scorpio is a water sign, it can share some broad traits with Cancer and Pisces, such as empathy or creativity. But Scorpio's water element is sometimes described as "fixed water" in astrology terms. "Fixed" refers to a stable, persistent quality. This means Scorpio's emotions and aims are less likely to shift quickly. Once they decide on a path, they tend to stay on it. Water that is fixed can be like a deep lake—calm on top, but with a lot going on below. This steady emotional core can help Scorpio stand firm, even when others around them may be uncertain.

One reason the water element fits Scorpio is that water can be hard to control. It flows where it needs to, and if you block it, it seeks another path. Scorpio individuals can show this trait. If they meet a barrier, they look for a different way to meet their goals. They do not usually give up just because something is in their way. Water also can wear down rocks over time. Scorpio's patience and staying power can resemble this slow but sure effect. Even if they must wait or plan carefully, they keep going until they find a solution.

Emotions are often a big part of water signs, and Scorpio is no exception. The difference is that Scorpio might not display these emotions for everyone to see. Because they tend to hold things inside, people around them might think they do not feel much. In truth, a Scorpio's emotional depth can be very strong, like an underwater current that is not obvious at first glance. This might be why some Scorpios are careful about who they trust. Once they open up, it becomes clear that their feelings can be powerful. The water element encourages this depth, giving Scorpio a steady well of emotion.

The water element also connects Scorpio to intuition. Water signs often rely on a sense of knowing or "gut feeling" about people and situations. Scorpio's version of intuition can be sharp and sometimes startlingly accurate. They might sense when something is off or when someone is not telling the whole truth. This ability is not magical; it often comes from paying close attention to small cues. Like water that flows into every crack, Scorpio's intuition can find tiny clues in a person's tone or body language. Though they might not always share these perceptions, they often sense more than others realize.

Scorpio's symbol and element combine to show a balance between the scorpion's outer defense and water's emotional, adaptable nature. The scorpion hints at self-protection, caution, and hidden power. The water element points to feeling, adaptability, and depth. Taken together, these qualities create a zodiac sign that can be both reserved and deeply caring, quiet on the surface but strong underneath. A Scorpio might appear calm and even distant at times, yet inside they can be moving through many layers of thoughts and emotions. The scorpion and the water element help us see how these traits fit together into a single astrological sign.

Many people like to wear or display Scorpio symbols in their homes. They might choose jewelry shaped like a scorpion or the zodiac glyph, or they might hang pictures that feature water themes to remind them of their sign. Some also pick colors like dark red, black, or deep purple, since these shades are often linked to Scorpio. These personal expressions connect back to the scorpion symbol and water element. Even people who are not deeply into astrology can feel drawn to the strong image of a scorpion or the mystery of deep water. It can be a fun way to identify with Scorpio's aura.

Because Scorpio is a water sign, they may find that activities involving water can bring them calm or even inspiration. Some Scorpios like to swim, relax by the sea, or take calming baths. Even just walking by a lake or river can make them feel more at ease. This is not a rule, but it fits with the idea that water might soothe Scorpio's strong emotional currents. Just as a scorpion naturally lives in hidden or shadowy places, a Scorpio might seek peaceful or private spots to think and reflect. Water, with its gentler sounds and waves, can be the perfect background for this.

There are also associations between Scorpio and certain stones or crystals. While these are not strictly part of mainstream science, some people enjoy linking zodiac signs to specific gems. For Scorpio, stones like obsidian, topaz, or malachite are sometimes mentioned because of their colors or supposed energies. Obsidian, for example, is black and shiny, reflecting the idea of hidden depth. Topaz can appear in deeper hues, matching Scorpio's strong feelings. Malachite has swirling green patterns that hint at transformation. Whether someone believes in the power of stones or not, these items remind us of Scorpio's focus on intensity, depth, and hidden layers.

Another element of Scorpio's water nature is emotional renewal. Just as water can clean and wash away dirt, Scorpio has the ability to work through heavy feelings and come out feeling refreshed. They might not do this in a public way, but they can find private methods to handle sadness, worry, or stress. If they trust someone, they might share what they are going through, but if not, they could write or spend quiet time alone until they feel better. The scorpion symbol in this case shows that they keep their personal struggles hidden. Only those who know them well see what is happening underneath.

Scorpio's link to water can also show up in their creative side. Some enjoy painting, drawing, or writing because these activities let them pour out their deep emotions in a safe way. Like water running through cracks, creativity can be a path for Scorpio to release strong feelings. In these forms of expression, the scorpion nature might show up as themes of mystery or hidden truths. Whether it is a painting with dark hues or a story filled with emotional tension, Scorpio can capture a sense of intensity. The water element encourages them to explore many levels of feeling without always speaking them aloud.

When thinking about the scorpion symbol, it is worth noting that not all Scorpios feel a special liking for the creature itself. Some might even fear or dislike scorpions in real life. The symbol is more about the qualities it represents than a literal wish to handle scorpions. The important idea is that a scorpion stays careful, strikes only when it feels necessary, and moves quietly in its environment. These points mirror some of Scorpio's emotional style. They can watch and wait, remain hidden, and then act when they see the right moment. The water element supports this approach by adding patience and adaptability.

The water element also suggests that Scorpio can relate to the waves of feeling that come from events in life. While others might quickly dismiss their feelings, Scorpio can linger on them, sensing every detail. This can help them understand complex emotional issues. The scorpion symbol might look tough, but water reminds us that there is a softer side too. This mix of tough exterior and sensitive interior can show up in how Scorpios bond with people. They might protect themselves behind a shell, yet once they trust someone, they can be very compassionate. The scorpion and water each reflect a different part of this dual nature.

CHAPTER 4: KEY STRENGTHS OF SCORPIO

Scorpio is known for a range of positive traits that set it apart from other zodiac signs. Though some people often focus on Scorpio's mystery, there are many clear strengths that can make a Scorpio stand out. One main strength is an impressive sense of resolve. When a Scorpio decides on a goal, they rarely back down. This can help them with tasks at school, projects at work, or challenges at home. Their drive does not fade easily, and they can keep pushing forward even when the task is tough. This level of commitment often surprises others who do not expect such tenacity.

Another big strength is Scorpio's sense of loyalty. Once they decide that someone matters to them, they can be very supportive. This does not mean they trust quickly, but once that trust is formed, it becomes a strong bond. Scorpio friends, family members, or partners are often the ones you can count on to help in hard times. They can keep secrets and offer real understanding when someone is upset or worried. This caring nature might not always show on the surface, but it is there for the people they value. This makes Scorpio a sign that can form deep, lasting connections.

Scorpio also shows skill in handling big emotional situations. While some people run from intense feelings, Scorpio can face them. They might not share these feelings right away, but they do not shy away from looking at complex emotional issues. This can be an advantage when dealing with family conflicts, tough friendships, or even personal struggles. A Scorpio's willingness to look at the full depth of feelings can help them find answers that others might miss. They do not mind examining the roots of a problem to understand what went wrong, and then they figure out the best way to move forward.

Bravery is another strength often linked to Scorpio. This does not always mean they are fearless in a physical sense. Rather, they can show courage in facing personal fears or helping someone through a scary time. They often have the inner steel to do what needs to be done, even if it is uncomfortable. A Scorpio might step up to defend a friend or stand by someone who is being treated unfairly. They could also display bravery by telling the truth when it would be easier to stay silent. This inner toughness helps them push through challenges that might overwhelm others.

Scorpios are also resourceful. When confronted with a problem, they tend to look for ways around it or through it. They do not usually give up just because something seems difficult. Instead, they might come up with creative solutions that others have not considered. This resourcefulness can come from their habit of paying close attention to details. They notice small facts that can be useful later. For instance, they might remember a piece of information from a conversation weeks ago and use it to solve a current issue. This skill can make them valuable in teamwork or in personal projects.

One of Scorpio's strengths is their ability to focus. When they pick a task that interests them, they can lose themselves in it for hours. This deep focus can lead to a high level of skill or knowledge. If a Scorpio wants to learn a new hobby, they might practice until they are quite advanced. They do not mind dedicating time to perfecting something they care about. In a school or work setting, this can help them finish projects with care. That same focus also means they do not get bored easily if they believe in the value of what they are doing.

Scorpios often show strength in handling responsibility. They might not want every task or job, but if they agree to do something, they usually mean it. They do not like to let people down or leave tasks half-finished. This can make them reliable leaders or helpers in group settings. If a Scorpio signs up for a role in a club or a community event, people can expect that they will take it seriously. This sense of responsibility also extends to personal relationships. If they promise to keep a friend's secret, they will do so, showing a level of trustworthiness that stands out.

Another strength is Scorpio's ability to plan. Because they observe details and think deeply about possible outcomes, they often excel at coming up with careful steps toward a goal. They do not usually rush blindly. Instead, they gather facts, consider options, and then choose a course of action. This planning skill can help them avoid mistakes. It can also give them confidence because they have thought of what could go wrong. While they do not always share their plans with everyone, they keep track of them in their mind. In a way, it is like a chess game, and Scorpios are good at thinking ahead.

Scorpios can also bring a special kind of empathy to their friendships and family ties. They might appear reserved, but when someone is in emotional pain, they can sense it. They are not afraid of big feelings, so they do not run away when a friend is upset. Instead, they might ask careful questions or simply offer silent support. Because they understand complex feelings in themselves, they can offer comfort without judging. This empathy is a powerful strength, allowing Scorpios to help others feel understood. It can lead to close, trusting relationships that last for years.

People born under Scorpio can show strong resolve when working on personal improvement. They do not necessarily talk about it openly, but they can push themselves to be better in certain areas of life. This might mean studying a new subject, improving a skill, or finding ways to manage anger or worry. Their sign's focus helps them stick to these efforts. Unlike those who might try something new and quit quickly, Scorpios tend to keep going until they see progress. This can lead them to develop talents that surprise others, because they worked quietly behind the scenes, guided by their own sense of purpose.

Scorpio's strong mind can be another advantage. Once they set their thoughts on solving a riddle or understanding a difficult topic, they put in the time to figure it out. They might enjoy research or puzzles because they love seeing how things fit together. In school, a Scorpio child might excel in subjects that require deep thinking. As adults, they may thrive in fields like analysis, investigation, or planning. Their minds are often sharp, and they enjoy sifting through information to find an answer. This mental strength stands out, as it pairs well with the sign's emotional insight.

A further strength is Scorpio's ability to remain calm when others are panicking. Of course, they do feel stress or worry, but they can hold it inside long enough to handle urgent tasks. This makes them good to have around in a crisis. They might not be the loudest person in the room, but they can keep a level head and think logically about what needs to be done. Afterward, they might feel the emotional impact, but in the moment, they are often able to step up. This quality can make others see them as strong, reliable, or even heroic.

Another positive trait is Scorpio's sense of fairness. They may feel upset if they see someone treated badly. They might also try to bring hidden information to light so that an issue can be fixed. Because they sense when something is wrong, they can be quick to notice injustice. If they have the power to help, they often do. This can be seen in how they stand up for friends or volunteer in causes that matter to them. Even though they might not shout their opinions, they have a solid moral code. This code can guide them when they decide what is right or wrong.

Scorpio's approach to honesty is another strong point. Many Scorpios value truth, even if it is uncomfortable. They might prefer to talk about important problems directly rather than pretend everything is fine. Though they do not reveal their own secrets easily, they can be straightforward when commenting on a situation. They often know that facing the truth can help everyone see what steps are needed. While their honesty can sometimes feel blunt, it is not usually meant to harm. Instead, it grows from their belief that facts matter. This can help them gain respect from people who value clear, honest talk.

Along with honesty, Scorpios can show a desire for real connections. They do not always enjoy small talk, but when they find someone who shares their interests, they can form a strong bond. They seek friends who are genuine, preferring depth over a large number of casual acquaintances. This can be a great strength in building lifelong friendships. People who form a bond with Scorpio often find they can trust them with personal information or rely on them in times of need. Scorpio's connections might be fewer but are often rooted in genuine care and respect, making them stable and meaningful.

Scorpios can also show creativity. Because of their sign's intensity, they might be drawn to art forms that allow deep self-expression, such as writing stories, composing music, or painting vivid pictures. They can pour strong emotions into their work, resulting in art that touches others on a sincere level. This creativity is a strength because it provides a way for Scorpios to channel feelings in a positive manner. It can help them manage stress or sadness. At the same time, it produces something that others can appreciate. Their art, no matter the form, often resonates with audiences who sense the real emotion behind it.

An additional strength is Scorpio's steadiness in personal routines or habits they care about. If they decide to exercise regularly, read every day, or keep a certain bedtime, they tend to stick with it. While not every Scorpio follows strict habits, many show a stubbornness that can help them maintain consistency. This can be very useful when trying to achieve long-term goals. They can set a schedule or personal rule and then follow it without needing constant reminders. This sense of self-discipline can grow stronger over time, giving them a firm foundation in areas like health, studies, or personal skills.

Scorpios can be protective of loved ones, which can be a major strength within a family or a close group of friends. If someone they care about is in danger or being treated poorly, they are likely to step in. They might not do it in a loud way, but they will find a method to defend or support that person. This protective spirit builds trust. Friends and family often know that Scorpio will not stand by if something unfair is happening. This sense of protection is tied to their loyalty, forming a strong bond within close circles.

Another strength is the sense of determination that many Scorpios show. This can apply to big life choices as well as smaller daily tasks. Whether it is finishing a tricky project at work, saving money for something important, or learning to fix things around the house, Scorpios do not easily quit once they set their mind on it. They look at the steps required and push through obstacles. If someone says a task is too hard, that can make Scorpio even more committed to doing it. This determination can inspire others, because they see that challenges can be overcome with enough focus and effort.

CHAPTER 5: KNOWN WEAKNESSES OF SCORPIO

Scorpios are often admired for their strong will and loyalty, but like all zodiac signs, they have weaknesses too. Understanding these weaker points can help people see why Scorpios might act in certain ways. One common issue is a tendency toward jealousy. When Scorpios become close to someone or value something, they might feel a strong need to protect that bond or item. If they sense a threat, they can feel jealous quickly. This can affect friendships, families, and even work settings. While it is not always clear on the outside, jealousy can simmer beneath the surface and cause inner stress.

Another known weakness is suspicion. Because Scorpios tend to observe and question what is going on, they might start to think that others have hidden motives. This can lead them to doubt people's words or actions more than necessary. In some cases, healthy caution is good, but too much suspicion can harm trust. A Scorpio might see a small comment or a tiny change in someone's behavior and think it means something bigger. This can cause them to withdraw or become guarded. If left unchecked, the need to watch for dishonest acts can create distance between Scorpio and the people they care about.

Scorpios can also hold onto grudges for a long time. This is partly because of their strong memory and deep emotional nature. If they feel hurt or betrayed, they may replay the event in their mind. This can make it hard for them to forgive and move on. While it is important not to forget serious harm, clinging to old wounds can weigh them down. Friends or family might be surprised when a

Scorpio brings up a small issue from long ago. This habit can block healing and make it tough for everyone to have a calm and open bond.

Some Scorpios have trouble with control, wanting to guide or manage situations, events, or people around them. Because they have a strong sense of direction, they might believe their approach is best. They can be very firm in trying to make sure everything goes as planned. But this can come across as pushy or controlling to those who prefer more freedom. In a group setting, Scorpio might appear bossy if they do not allow space for other ideas. Over time, controlling behaviors can strain personal bonds, especially when friends or partners want their own views respected.

Scorpios can be private, which is not always a weakness. But it becomes one if they shut out the people closest to them. They might keep secrets or hide feelings for fear of being hurt or misunderstood. This can lead to misunderstandings because others do not know what Scorpio is thinking or feeling. In friendships, it might look like Scorpio does not trust anyone enough to share. In a family, it can cause confusion when a Scorpio child or adult refuses to talk about an important event. Keeping everything locked inside can build pressure and create emotional distance.

Another area of concern is moodiness. With strong feelings moving beneath the surface, Scorpios might go from calm to upset quickly. A small event can trigger strong emotion if it touches on a sensitive topic or fear. Because they do not always show these feelings openly, it can be hard for others to predict Scorpio's reactions. This can cause confusion for friends or co-workers who do not realize a shift is happening. If Scorpio's moods swing too often, it can disrupt daily life. Learning to spot the signs of an oncoming mood change can help them manage it more smoothly.

In some cases, Scorpios may use manipulation, especially if they feel cornered. They might try to control outcomes by nudging people in certain directions or withholding information. This does not mean all Scorpios are manipulative, but the potential is there due to their deep understanding of emotions and motivations. If they sense someone might be working against them, they could respond by being less direct and more strategic. Over time, manipulative actions can damage trust, because people prefer honesty. Scorpios who catch themselves doing this can help matters by speaking up more openly and checking their own motives.

Perfectionism can also be a problem. Scorpios, with their keen eye and focus, might set very high standards for themselves and others. While striving for quality is not bad, it can become stressful if they cannot accept normal human errors. A Scorpio might push themselves to keep going long after they are tired, or they might criticize small mistakes in a group project. This can lead to tension and stress for everyone. Perfectionism might make them feel they are never good enough or that others are letting them down. Recognizing when to ease up can help them find a healthier balance.

A related weakness is a fear of failure. Since Scorpios often put their heart into their tasks, they might dread the idea of falling short. This fear can hold them back from taking healthy risks or trying new things. They might avoid situations where they are not sure they can succeed. It can also make them defensive if someone points out a flaw or error in their work. Instead of seeing it as a chance to improve, they may take it personally. Finding ways to see mistakes as learning points can help Scorpios move past the fear of not doing well.

Some Scorpios feel drawn to intense experiences and strong emotions. While this can be exciting, it can also lead them into unbalanced highs and lows. This might mean they get bored with calm periods in life and seek drama or conflict, even without realizing it. In relationships, a Scorpio might feel that real passion only appears through big emotional moments. This can be draining for everyone involved. Also, constantly craving intensity can cause them to miss out on quiet but meaningful joys. Recognizing that steady, positive moments are valuable can help them avoid chasing tension that is not truly needed.

Because of their suspicious nature, some Scorpios might test people as a way to feel safe. For instance, they may ask a friend several questions to see if the friend is telling the truth or watch how someone acts under a bit of pressure. While checking trust is understandable, doing it too often can strain a relationship. The other person might sense they are being examined, which can feel unfair. Scorpio might believe they are just being careful, but to others it can feel like a lack of faith. This habit can make close connections more complicated than they need to be.

Scorpios can struggle with letting go of the past. This is slightly different from holding grudges. Even if they are not angry anymore, they might still hold onto regrets or sadness from old events. They can replay scenarios in their mind and wonder what went wrong. While reflection can be helpful, too much dwelling can keep them from focusing on better days ahead. It can also cause them to doubt their own worth if they see past mistakes as permanent marks. Finding healthy ways to move forward can free them from being stuck in old thoughts that no longer serve a purpose.

In group settings, Scorpio's drive and determination can come across as stubbornness. While it is admirable to stick to one's views, sometimes a more flexible approach would be better. But Scorpios can dig in their heels if they truly believe in something. This might lead to arguments, especially if teammates or family members prefer compromise. Being open to other ideas can help Scorpios grow. If they refuse to budge at all, they risk missing out on new viewpoints. Over time, others might see them as uncooperative, which can harm both personal and professional connections.

Some Scorpios have a hidden fear of exposure. They do not want their secrets or vulnerabilities revealed. While privacy is normal, this can become a problem if it leads them to push people away. They might avoid close friendships or romantic connections because they are afraid of being truly seen. This could create a lonely feeling, even if they do not admit it. Also, if someone accidentally sees a side of them that they wanted to hide, they might react with anger or deny it. Working on self-acceptance can help ease this fear, letting them build closer, more honest bonds.

Scorpios can also be quite direct in pointing out issues or flaws in others. While honesty is typically a good trait, the way it is delivered matters. If Scorpio shares these views with too much force, it can come across as harsh. This can hurt feelings or cause people to become defensive. Over time, friends or family might dread hearing Scorpio's opinions if they are always sharply presented. Finding softer ways to communicate can reduce tension. A well-chosen phrase or a more gentle tone can still convey truth but in a way that is easier for others to accept and consider.

Another tricky weakness is the urge for revenge. Most Scorpios do not act on this in extreme ways, but they might entertain thoughts of getting even if they believe someone has harmed them. Because they feel emotions strongly, the idea of justice or payback can be tempting. Even small slights might linger in their mind, leading them to dwell on how to even the score. This can poison their peace of mind and cause negativity in their environment. Letting go of the desire for payback can free them from carrying anger that does more harm to them than to anyone else.

Some Scorpios can be impatient when they want things done their way. Their strong will pushes them to achieve results quickly, but life does not always move at the same speed. If a Scorpio is in charge of a project, they may become irritated if others work at a slower pace. They might snap at team members or try to do everything themselves. In family situations, impatience can show up when children or siblings do not follow instructions right away. Learning to manage this urge for instant outcomes can help reduce stress. A bit of patience can make teamwork more pleasant.

In romantic relationships, Scorpio's intensity can sometimes flip into possessiveness. If they worry about losing someone, they might try to keep an eye on their partner's activities or friendships. They could ask many questions or want frequent updates, leading the partner to feel restricted. Over time, this can destroy trust, which is the opposite of what Scorpio wants. Recognizing that healthy boundaries are vital for both people in the relationship can prevent this possessive streak from taking over. It can be challenging, but giving loved ones room to breathe can actually strengthen the bond in the long run.

Scorpios might also underestimate the importance of showing small signs of kindness or warmth. Because they are often deep thinkers, they can focus on major matters and forget that little gestures are important too. This lack of outward warmth can make them seem distant. They might not realize that a tiny smile, a friendly greeting, or a gentle word can go a long way in making others feel valued. People who do not see these small acts may believe Scorpio does not care. Working on outward expression can help Scorpios connect better with friends, family, and co-workers.

CHAPTER 6: SCORPIO & FEELINGS

Scorpio is often called one of the most emotionally intense signs. This means they experience feelings with great depth and strength. Even when they appear calm, they might be grappling with complex emotions inside. Because they are a water sign, their feelings can flow in powerful currents. Many people sense a certain depth when talking to a Scorpio, as if there is more happening beneath the surface than meets the eye. This can make Scorpios good at understanding serious topics, but it can also mean they might hold onto strong feelings for longer than some other signs do.

One notable aspect of Scorpio feelings is the pull toward secrecy. They often do not broadcast their moods or invite everyone into their emotional world. They might share surface-level details with acquaintances, while keeping deeper emotions for a small circle of trusted people. This can make them seem tough or closed-off. In reality, it is just how they protect themselves. When they do decide to open up, they can surprise people with how much they have been carrying inside. This private style means their emotional world is well-guarded, which can be both a strength and a barrier to closer bonds.

Scorpios tend to feel a wide range of emotions, from extreme happiness to deep sadness. They rarely settle in mild, middle ground. If they are excited, they can be very enthusiastic, pouring energy into a creative project or showing great warmth to the people close to them. But if they are unhappy, the feeling can run just as deep in the opposite direction. They might withdraw, leaving friends or family confused about what went wrong. This intensity can be hard for some people to handle, but it is part of what makes Scorpios capable of empathy and strong passion.

Due to their powerful emotional nature, Scorpios can sense subtle clues in others. They often notice small changes in tone or facial expression. This can help them figure out when a friend is feeling worried or sad, even if that person has not said so. In a family setting, a Scorpio child might pick up on tension between adults before anyone else acknowledges it. While this can be helpful for understanding those around them, it can also weigh heavily on Scorpio's mind. They might absorb the feelings in a room, leading them to feel overloaded if the mood is negative.

Scorpios tend to form very strong emotional bonds once they let someone in. They might choose only a few close friends or family members to trust fully. But with those chosen few, their feelings run deep. They might remember little details from years ago, or quietly support someone going through a crisis. Because they invest so much in these connections, they can be deeply affected if anything goes wrong. This is part of why betrayal feels especially painful to them. They do not take closeness lightly, so losing trust can hurt them in a major way.

Romance for a Scorpio can be a powerful emotional field. When they care about someone, they tend to show strong devotion. However, their intense feelings can sometimes lead to worries about betrayal or dishonesty. If they sense something is off, they might feel upset even if nothing has truly gone wrong. This can cause tension in relationships if the partner does not understand Scorpio's need for emotional security. On the positive side, Scorpios can bring deep warmth, loyalty, and understanding to a romance. They can form bonds that feel very special to both people involved.

In family life, a Scorpio's emotions can color daily interactions. If a Scorpio child is upset, they might pout or withdraw until they feel ready to talk. If a Scorpio parent feels stressed, they might become quiet and serious, causing the rest of the family to worry. Clear communication can help address these shifts before they turn into bigger problems. Family members who learn to recognize signs of Scorpio's moods can offer support or space as needed. Over time, a well-understood Scorpio can become the emotional pillar of the family, sensing hidden problems and guiding others toward understanding.

Scorpios also have an emotional connection to their goals and passions. They throw themselves into tasks that spark strong feelings. This can be anything from art to volunteer work, as long as it resonates with their inner world. When they commit to something, they might spend hours researching, practicing, or improving. This emotional commitment can lead to success, but it can also leave them feeling drained if they do not manage their energy. Understanding how to pace themselves can help Scorpios avoid emotional burnout. Even though they love to dive deep into what they care about, breaks and rest are key.

Anger can be strong for a Scorpio. They do not always shout or rage in an obvious way, but the emotional force can be immense. If they feel betrayed or see something as unjust, they might boil inside. Some Scorpios try to hide it, but their frustration can leak out in short, pointed statements or an icy silence. If the anger grows, it can burst out in a more direct confrontation. Handling this emotion in a healthy way takes skill. Activities like writing, physical exercise, or talking with a trusted friend might help them release anger before it becomes too overwhelming.

On the other side of the emotional scale, Scorpios can feel deep affection. When they care about someone, they can express it in private, sincere ways—perhaps through a thoughtful favor or by defending that person against criticism. They might not always show big public displays, but the emotion is real and lasting. Because they are selective about who they form close bonds with, that affection can be powerful. Friends or family might sense that when a Scorpio says they love or care, they mean it. This honest emotional tone is one reason many value Scorpio's presence in their lives.

Fear can also play a role in Scorpio's emotional world, though they might not admit it. They can worry about losing loved ones, being betrayed, or failing in their aims. These fears sometimes lie under the surface and can drive their actions. For example, if a Scorpio fears that a friend might leave them, they might become overly protective or jealous. Understanding the root fear can help them manage the behavior. If they learn to trust both themselves and the people around them, they can ease these hidden anxieties. Recognizing that not everyone is out to hurt them can help them relax.

Scorpios can have a reflective relationship with sadness. When loss or disappointment hits, they might mourn it deeply, replaying the events in their mind. This can lead to a desire to understand the cause. They often need a bit of alone time to process these heavier emotions. Music, writing, or other forms of quiet reflection can help them let go of sadness. Because of their depth, they can handle dark moods, but it is healthier if they do not stay in that place too long. Having a supportive person to confide in can help them find comfort and eventually move forward.

Stress can have a big impact on Scorpio's feelings. Their strong focus can cause them to feel tense if there are too many demands. They might feel pressured at school or work, then bring that stress home. Because they are not always open about their struggles, friends or family might sense something is wrong but not know what. Scorpios can manage stress by actively finding outlets. This could involve hobbies, spending time in nature, or talking with someone they trust. Naming the stress can reduce its power. Acknowledging they need help sometimes does not make them weak; it can actually make them healthier.

Scorpios might also show a thoughtful nature in how they connect with others' feelings. They can offer a listening ear or quiet guidance to someone who is upset. Their ability to pick up on emotional undercurrents makes them skilled at soothing or advising friends. However, they must be careful not to absorb too much of others' sorrow or anger, as it can weigh them down. Setting boundaries helps them remain supportive without losing themselves in someone else's problems. When they learn to keep emotional balance, they can be a source of real comfort and understanding, thanks to their sensitive approach.

Self-awareness can help Scorpios handle their emotions better. Taking time to reflect on what they feel and why can lead to better control. Some might keep a journal or speak with a counselor to understand their emotional patterns. They might think about times when they felt angry or jealous and ask what caused those reactions. By digging into these triggers, Scorpios can figure out healthier responses. Over time, they can learn that not every feeling needs to be acted on right away. In this way, they can use their emotional depth in a way that benefits themselves and the people around them.

When Scorpios share their emotions, it can be a powerful moment for them and for those who hear it. Since they keep things inside, opening up can bring a sense of closeness. A Scorpio might decide to tell a friend about their fears, or share with a sibling how much they appreciate support. This vulnerability can feel risky, but it also allows them to form deeper, healthier bonds. Friends might realize how strongly a Scorpio values them. Family members might understand that the Scorpio is not as distant as they seemed. Such conversations can lead to growth in trust and respect.

Scorpios can also benefit from creative outlets. Art, music, writing, and similar forms of expression let them explore feelings without having to talk openly. They might write poems or songs that show a side of their emotions they cannot easily put into regular conversation. Some Scorpios discover they are good at painting or drawing scenes that capture the depths of what they feel. These outlets can help them transform powerful emotions into something meaningful. By doing this, they can prevent emotional overload and even create works that inspire or comfort others who see or hear them.

One key part of Scorpio's emotional life is learning to trust others enough to share what they are experiencing. Scorpios often worry about being hurt if they open up, but remaining silent can create misunderstandings. Friends and family might guess incorrectly about what is wrong. Over time, this can lead to arguments or confusion. Although it can be hard, finding people who have shown honesty in the past can encourage Scorpios to speak up. A gentle approach can make it simpler to say, "I'm feeling worried," or, "I'm scared about this situation." Honesty can protect them from the harm of unshared burdens.

Emotional honesty also helps Scorpios manage conflicts more effectively. If they are upset with a friend or partner, hiding it can cause the emotion to build. In time, it might explode in an argument. Addressing small problems early can prevent bigger clashes. A simple chat can be enough to clear the air if done calmly. Of course, it takes courage to admit feeling hurt or disappointed. But facing these feelings head-on is more constructive than pretending everything is fine. Over time, this approach can reduce the kind of suspicion or jealousy that arises when communication is not direct and clear.

In closing, Scorpio's emotional life is full of power and depth. They can feel everything strongly, both good and bad. While this can lead to challenges like jealousy or fear, it also allows them to show great empathy and devotion. By learning to trust, share, and manage stress, Scorpios can use their feelings in a positive way. They can form meaningful bonds, support others, and create insightful work that reflects their inner world. Emotions, for Scorpio, are not just passing states—they are core parts of who they are. When guided by understanding and honesty, these feelings can enrich their lives and the lives of those around them.

CHAPTER 7: SCORPIO AS A FRIEND

When you first meet a Scorpio, you might notice they are polite but a bit reserved. This can give the impression that they do not want to be close friends. In many cases, it only means they like to watch and learn about others before letting down their guard. A Scorpio will often focus quietly on the group, noticing small details and remembering them. If you see a Scorpio child in a new classroom, they might stand at the edge of the group, quietly listening. Later, when they feel more relaxed, they may start talking. This steady approach can shape many of their friendships.

Scorpios tend to be cautious when forming bonds. They do not hand out their trust easily. This is why some people say that befriending a Scorpio can take more time. Yet, once a Scorpio decides someone is trustworthy, they can form one of the most lasting connections. They value honesty and respect in their friendships. If you want a Scorpio friend to open up, showing genuine kindness is a good first step. Scorpios dislike forced or fake conversations. They would rather share a few real words than many empty phrases. Their guarded start is just part of finding true companionship.

One of the strongest traits of a Scorpio friend is loyalty. When they call you a friend, they mean it. They are not the type to pretend. If you are going through a tough time, they will often be the one quietly checking on you, offering help in their own way. This might be a simple text, a heartfelt talk, or even just showing up when you need company. They keep their promises because letting a friend down goes against their core values. Knowing that a Scorpio is in your corner can feel reassuring, especially when life gets complicated or uncertain.

A Scorpio friend also places high value on respect. If they sense a friend is being dishonest or sneaky, they may withdraw. While they understand that mistakes happen, they do not like feeling misled. If a friend apologizes sincerely, many Scorpios will forgive, though they might not forget. Their memory can be very sharp. This can be both good and bad. It is good because they remember nice things you said or did. It can be bad if you hurt them, because they might recall the details for a long time. Earning and keeping their respect is key to staying close.

Because Scorpios tend to observe rather than jump in, they can be excellent listeners. In a friendly chat, a Scorpio might stay silent, letting their friend share problems. Then, they offer thoughtful remarks. They try not to judge but will be honest if asked for an opinion. Their advice might be direct, which can feel blunt to some people. Yet, they usually give it out of care. If you have a Scorpio friend, you may notice they remember small bits of your story. Days or weeks later, they might bring up those details to ask if you feel better or if something has changed.

In groups, a Scorpio friend might seem like the quieter one at first. They do not always talk for the sake of talking. Instead, they speak up when they have something meaningful to add. If the group is loud and chatty, Scorpio might watch the flow of conversation to see who is sincere and who just wants attention. Over time, they choose which people they really connect with. Once they bond with a group, they can be a strong presence, supporting group goals. They can even become a peacemaker if disagreements come up, because they tend to sense hidden feelings and can guide everyone to talk honestly.

Scorpios take secrets seriously. If you tell a Scorpio friend something in confidence, they usually keep it close. They recognize the importance of trust and do not want to violate it. Because of this, many people feel safe talking to Scorpio about private topics. However, this works both ways. A Scorpio might not share their own secrets until they feel certain you will treat them with the same care. If you slip up and reveal a Scorpio's secret, it can cause deep hurt. Rebuilding that trust can be hard. They might still be polite, but the special closeness may be lost.

Some Scorpios show their care through small but meaningful acts. They may not always say, "I appreciate you," in words. Instead, they might help you with a task, remember your favorite snack, or check on you when you have a big exam. These thoughtful gestures are their way of saying, "I care." Scorpio might also surprise you by recalling a conversation from weeks back, proving they were listening. If you want to show you value a Scorpio friend, paying attention to their subtle hints can help. They often expect the same level of thought and care they give to others.

Conflict can arise in any friendship, and a Scorpio friend may handle it with strong emotion. If they feel wronged, they might be quiet at first, but inside they could be quite upset. A Scorpio does not always share immediate anger. They often think about what happened and decide how they feel before speaking. When they do address the issue, it can be straightforward. This honesty can catch people off guard if they were not prepared. It helps to remain calm and truthful. A Scorpio can handle tough topics, but they dislike being lied to or dismissed. With respect, many conflicts can be resolved.

Patience can be key when you have a Scorpio friend. They do not rush into lighthearted closeness. They like to see how you behave in different situations. For example, do you keep your word? Are you fair to others? Do you show genuine kindness? When they see consistent good traits, they feel safer opening up. This might mean you have to wait a while before hearing Scorpio's deeper thoughts. But the wait can be worth it. Once you are inside their trusted circle, you might find that Scorpio is a faithful supporter who will stand by you when everyone else steps away.

Because Scorpio's emotions run deep, they can offer comforting support when you are sad or stressed. They tend to understand heavy feelings, so they will not run off if you are upset. Instead, they might ask careful questions or quietly sit with you so you do not feel alone. They do not mind facing serious topics, and this allows them to be there for friends who are dealing with hard problems. However, this empathy also means Scorpio needs time to recharge. Taking on a friend's troubles can be draining. A thoughtful friend will realize that Scorpio also needs understanding and rest.

Sometimes, a Scorpio friend can have a protective streak. If they believe someone is treating you unfairly, they might step in with pointed words or actions. This can feel both reassuring and intense. Scorpio's protective side can be strong because they hold loyalty in high regard. Be aware that if you do not actually want or need help, you may need to tell Scorpio gently. They can be so focused on defending a friend that they forget not everyone handles conflict the same way. Still, this protective nature is often a sign of their deep care, and many friends feel grateful for it.

Scorpios are not always comfortable with superficial chatter. If a group is talking about small topics just to pass the time, Scorpio might become quiet or bored. They prefer deeper conversations about real interests, emotions, or ideas. If you want to connect with a Scorpio friend, try discussing topics that matter to both of you. It could be books, movies, personal goals, or events that made you think. This does not mean Scorpios never laugh or share silly moments. They do, but they also want substance in their friendships.

Providing that substance can help your bond grow stronger and more genuine.

When Scorpios are younger, they might show some of these friendship traits in simpler forms. A Scorpio child might cling to one or two close playmates, being extra watchful around kids they do not trust yet. A teen Scorpio might be a loyal friend who keeps secrets and stands up for classmates, but also can become withdrawn if hurt. Learning to talk about their feelings is an important step for young Scorpios. If they grow up in an environment where open communication is valued, they can develop healthy ways of dealing with any fear or suspicion. Friends who show patience can help them learn to share more.

A Scorpio friend might be selective about where they spend their time. They often prefer calm or private hangouts rather than very loud or crowded places. This does not mean they never enjoy parties; they might, especially if they know and trust the people there. But they tend to feel more at ease in smaller groups. If you invite a Scorpio friend to a big event, they might hang back at first, scanning the crowd. If they spot a close friend, they may stay close to that person. They appreciate having at least one solid connection in any large gathering.

Humor can be an interesting part of a Scorpio friendship. Some Scorpios have a quick, playful wit. They might tease their friends lightly, but it usually does not come from a mean place. Instead, it is a way to show closeness. Still, their humor can be sharp or dry, so friends should understand that is just Scorpio's style. If they sense a friend is sensitive, they might go easier with jokes. Scorpio also appreciates honesty in humor, so fake compliments or forced laughter is not something they enjoy. They would rather share a real laugh over something genuinely funny or clever.

Scorpios often keep track of birthdays or special occasions for the people they care about. They might not plan a big event, but they will remember and often do something thoughtful. For example, a Scorpio friend might write a heartfelt card or give a carefully chosen gift. This gesture can show their friend they are important. Because Scorpio notices details, they might recall you once mentioned a favorite snack, book, or color. Then, they surprise you with something related to that detail. It is their way of saying, "I pay attention to what matters to you," which can feel very sincere.

In a crisis, a Scorpio friend can be a stable force. They often stay calm or at least appear calm on the outside, which helps them think clearly. Even if they feel worry inside, they tend to focus on what needs to be done. Friends might call on Scorpio when they need a plan or a reliable helper. Scorpio can quickly gather facts, consider the best steps, and take action. This could be something big, like helping a friend move out of a difficult living situation, or something smaller, like comforting someone who received bad news. They see it as their duty to help if they can.

Misunderstandings can happen when Scorpio's quiet nature is mistaken for disinterest. Some friends might think Scorpio does not care because they do not talk a lot about their own thoughts. Others might see Scorpio's direct advice as harsh. If you have a Scorpio friend, remember that their form of kindness can be subtle, and their honesty is usually meant to help, not hurt. If you are unsure about something they said, asking calmly for clarity can resolve problems. Scorpios appreciate open dialogue, even if it is a bit uncomfortable. Avoiding the issue might allow suspicion or tension to grow.

Trust can be the biggest factor in a Scorpio friendship. They might test this trust over time. This does not mean they play games or tricks, but they do pay attention to how you handle sensitive information. They also watch how you treat other people. If you are loyal, fair, and true to your word, Scorpio will see that. Over many shared experiences, their trust deepens. Once a Scorpio really trusts you, they might reveal more about their personal life, their feelings, or their dreams. This is a sign of deep friendship with a Scorpio: they allow you behind the walls they keep up for most people.

It can help to learn about a Scorpio friend's interests to strengthen your bond. Scorpios often enjoy topics like mysteries, science, deep storytelling, or anything that challenges the mind. If you show genuine curiosity, they might share recommendations for books, shows, or games they enjoy. This can spark conversations that let them open up more. They also appreciate friends who bring them new ideas. If you introduce a Scorpio to a new puzzle or a thoughtful film, they might be grateful. These moments can create a sense of shared discovery, helping the friendship grow deeper over time.

Sometimes, a Scorpio friend might vanish for a bit, especially if they feel overwhelmed. They could take some time alone to process problems. This might seem like a sudden retreat. If this happens, try not to take it as rejection. Many Scorpios need space to regain emotional balance. A kind message to let them know you are there for them can help. They may not respond right away, but they often appreciate the gesture. When they come back, they might be more ready to talk. Giving them room to handle their feelings shows respect, which is something Scorpios value highly.

Scorpios can be passionate about fairness. If they see a friend being treated poorly, they may encourage that friend to stand up for themselves. They might even step in if the situation is serious. Because they notice unspoken details, they can sense when a friend is not speaking up about a problem. They could say something like, "I can tell you're upset. Do you want to talk?" This caring approach can help friends feel understood. On the other hand, if Scorpio believes a friend is in the wrong, they might say so. This directness can prevent long-term issues if handled respectfully.

A Scorpio friend can sometimes seem mysterious because they do not reveal every part of themselves. They might share one side of their life but keep another side private. Friends might see them as full of contradictions—warm one day, distant the next. This can be confusing, but it is part of Scorpio's layered personality. If you value that friend, offering patience and asking open-ended questions can encourage them to share more. Simply saying, "I'm here whenever you want to talk," can mean a lot. Over time, as trust builds, a Scorpio may show the calmer, more open aspects of their nature.

Because Scorpios put so much energy into close friendships, they might not have a large circle of companions. Instead, they focus on a few important people. This does not make them unfriendly, but they are selective. They prefer genuine bonds over large groups of acquaintances. If you find yourself in that inner circle, you may notice they stay loyal even if distance or time changes circumstances. A Scorpio might reach out after months of little contact just to check if you are okay. That kind of thoughtful loyalty can be surprising, but it shows how strongly they value the people they have chosen.

Encouraging a Scorpio friend can go a long way. They often appear confident, but they can doubt themselves at times, especially if they fear failing. A sincere compliment or a few words of support might boost their morale more than you realize. They respect honest praise. Flattery that sounds fake will not impress them. Letting them know you see their hard work or their unique talents can deepen the bond. They might also appreciate someone noticing their quiet kindness. Because Scorpios do not always show vulnerabilities, a few caring words can reassure them that they are not alone in whatever they face.

Communication styles can differ among zodiac signs, but with Scorpio, direct yet respectful speech often works best. They do not enjoy mind games or indirect hints. If you have an issue, calmly stating it usually gains a better response than dropping vague clues. Likewise, if they say something that confuses you, asking politely for more information can clear things up. Both sides benefit from honesty, which Scorpio regards as essential. They prefer a difficult truth over a kind lie. In the long run, sticking to the facts and showing you care about genuine understanding can keep the friendship steady.

Some Scorpios love deep, thoughtful chats about life, the universe, or even topics like dreams and human nature. If you share these interests, you might find yourself talking with a Scorpio friend for hours. They can be good at examining different angles of a subject, and they respect friends who can do the same. On the flip side, if a person only wants to talk about shallow gossip or brag about themselves, Scorpio might lose interest. They do not mind a bit of casual talk, but they thrive on deeper connections. Their best friendships often center on shared curiosity and personal growth.

Practical support is another way a Scorpio friend shows they care. If you are moving to a new apartment, they may offer to pack boxes or drive a truck. If you have an important exam, they might help you study. They see friendship as more than just fun outings. Taking real action to help a friend is part of their loyalty. This does not mean they want praise or attention for their help. They usually do not. They simply believe that if you are a true friend, you show up when needed. Over time, people often remember these helpful acts as a mark of Scorpio's lasting friendship.

Scorpios can also sense when a friend might be hiding true feelings. They are good at reading body language, tone of voice, or even pauses in conversation. If you try to pretend you are fine while you are actually upset, a Scorpio might gently ask if something is bothering you. If you say "no" but your demeanor suggests otherwise, they might keep watching to see if you need support. They will not always push you to talk, but they remember what they notice. You might find them asking about it later, once they think you are ready to open up.

It is important to note that Scorpios can also expect friends to respect their personal space. Even though they observe others, they might not appreciate someone constantly pushing them to spill private thoughts. If a Scorpio says they do not want to talk about something right now, it is wise to respect that boundary. Pressuring them might cause them to pull away more. Over time, they might share when they feel safe enough. Balancing genuine concern with the patience to let them reveal things at their own pace can keep the friendship solid. Rushing them can make them wary and guarded.

In times of shared joy, a Scorpio friend can be quietly happy for you. They might not always show excitement with big gestures, but they can smile or offer heartfelt words. They pay attention to the important events in your life, be it a new job, an award, or even a small success that matters to you. A sincere "I'm proud of you" from a Scorpio can carry a lot of meaning. Because they do not say such things lightly, you know they mean it. They might also offer practical help or advice to keep your good fortune going strong.

Scorpio's determined spirit can influence their friendships. If they set a goal for the two of you—like finishing a shared project, joining a sports team, or learning a new skill—they will push to see it through. This can be motivating but also demanding. They might expect the same level of commitment from you. If you do not share their enthusiasm, disagreements could arise. Talking about each person's limits and hopes at the start can help. That way, no one feels pressured. When you do share the same drive, you might form a remarkable team. Scorpio's focus combined with your support can lead to strong results.

Some Scorpios might struggle to ask for help directly, even from good friends. Their independent streak can be strong, and they might believe they should handle problems alone. If you notice a Scorpio friend looks stressed or distant, asking gently if they need a hand can open the door. They might turn you down at first out of pride or habit. Still, letting them know the offer is real might encourage them later. Because they usually care a lot about fairness, if you help them, they may want to return the favor. This mutual support can deepen the friendship bond.

In a friend circle, Scorpio might be the one who remembers birthdays or small moments that others forget. They often keep mental notes of friends' likes and dislikes. If someone in the group has special dietary needs, Scorpio might make sure the restaurant you all pick has good options for that person. These thoughtful acts show how they value harmony and comfort among friends. They do not always say, "I did this for you," because they do not seek applause. They just consider it normal to help. Such care can make them a beloved member of the friend circle who quietly helps hold things together.

Scorpios usually value honesty in how they speak about friends when they are not around. They dislike gossip that aims to tear someone down. If they have concerns, they prefer to address them directly or keep them private. This does not mean they never talk about people, but they try to avoid harmful rumors. If they hear false stories about a friend, they might step in to correct them. Scorpio can be protective of a friend's reputation, especially if that friend is not present to defend themselves. Their sense of fairness pushes them to speak up when they think something is wrong.

Some Scorpios can be competitive, even with friends. This does not always mean they want to beat you in a game or test. Rather, they might strive to improve themselves and compare their progress with others. If they see a friend doing well, they might feel challenged to do better too. In a healthy friendship, this can spark mutual growth. You can cheer each other on while pushing each other forward. In an unhealthy setting, it might cause envy. Good communication can prevent issues. If both friends understand they are each other's allies, that friendly competition can be fun instead of tense.

Handling a Scorpio's strong emotions can be tricky for friends. If a Scorpio feels sorrow, betrayal, or anger, it can run deep. They might want to shut themselves away for a while. If you sense this happening, offering quiet support without prying can help. You could send a kind note or suggest a calm activity, giving them an option to say yes or no. Over time, many Scorpios learn to balance their emotions so they do not hurt their friendships. But if they are still learning, patience from the friend side is important. Remind them that you are there if they want to talk.

Scorpios can also be quite private about money or personal resources, but they will be generous if a friend is in true need. If they see someone they care about in a difficult situation, they might quietly offer a loan or share what they have. They rarely boast about helping, so others might not even know. This hidden generosity comes from their view that real friendship includes care in all areas of life, including practical needs. If they sense someone is trying to take advantage, however, they will shut down immediately. Trust is vital, and they expect gratitude or fairness in return.

Because Scorpio can handle emotional depth, they often connect well with friends who also appreciate sincerity. If you prefer only light, cheerful conversations, you might find Scorpio too serious. But if you enjoy sharing real stories and listening to deeper truths,

Scorpio can be an amazing match. The sign's water element makes them sensitive, while their fixed quality makes them steady. This mix can lead to a friendship that grows over time. Even if you do not share all the same interests, Scorpio's ability to listen and support can add a lot of richness to the bond you share.

A Scorpio friend may prefer quiet celebrations or gatherings rather than huge parties. They like events where they can talk with a few close companions. They want to connect on a personal level rather than spend the entire time making small talk. If you plan something for them, keeping it relaxed and meaningful might suit them more than an enormous public event. Some Scorpios do enjoy big get-togethers, but they usually want to have a comfortable spot or group where they can retreat if things become too loud. Providing that option can make them more relaxed and open during the event.

Over time, friendships with Scorpio can transform as they learn more about you and as you learn about them. In the early stages, they might appear somewhat distant or serious. Later, you might see a lighter side, complete with jokes and playful moments. Scorpios do not abandon their serious side, but they can show warmth once they feel safe. They might share funny stories about their life or send humorous texts. This shift is often a sign that they trust you. Cherishing these lighthearted moments can bring balance to the friendship, especially since Scorpios also have that deep, intense side.

Scorpios are known to stay up late talking with a friend if the topic is meaningful. They can lose track of time when discussing important issues, dreams, or problems. If you have a late-night conversation with a Scorpio, you might be surprised at how awake they seem, even in the early hours. Their focus can be strong, and they do not like to stop until they feel they have reached some understanding. This can be wonderful if you need someone to really hear you out.

Just be aware that they might expect the same attention if they decide to share their own worries or hopes.

In cases where a Scorpio feels a friend has broken their trust, the friendship may fade quickly. They might quietly distance themselves, not giving a big speech or argument. Instead, they simply become less available. Attempts to reconnect might be met with polite but cool responses. If you suspect this is happening, it might help to apologize or explain the situation honestly. Sometimes, they can forgive if they see genuine regret and changed behavior. However, if the damage seems too big, they might let the friendship go. This can be sad, but it comes from their deep need for honesty and fairness.

Scorpio friendships often grow stronger over shared experiences. If you tackle a difficult project together or travel through challenging conditions, Scorpio might bond more deeply because they see how you handle stress. A friend who stands firm during tough times can earn a special place in Scorpio's heart. They realize that a person who remains loyal under pressure is rare. They, in turn, will do their best to support you in your struggles. This can create a team spirit between you, turning random experiences into treasured memories. Scorpio is likely to recall these moments for years, holding them as proof of true friendship.

Another feature of Scorpio as a friend is their tendency to defend your reputation. If someone speaks poorly of you, Scorpio may step in with a calm but firm approach. They might correct misinformation or ask the person to reconsider their words. This defense happens more often when Scorpio feels sure about your character. They do not want to waste energy on someone who might actually be dishonest. But if they trust you, they will stand up for you. This loyalty can be comforting. However, it also means Scorpios expect you to be truthful with them, so they do not find themselves in a tricky spot.

Supporting a Scorpio friend is not just about cheering them on. It also involves respecting their need for alone time. If you try to be around them constantly or demand immediate replies to messages, they may feel overwhelmed. A balanced approach works best: showing interest but giving them space. If they vanish from social events for a bit, they might just need to recharge. Sending a simple note like, "Thinking of you, hope you're okay," can be enough to let them know they are not forgotten. Most Scorpios appreciate that you remember them without pushing too hard.

If a Scorpio friend has a creative hobby or passion, you might see a whole other side of them. They can become very enthusiastic while talking about their favorite topic. Whether it is painting, writing, playing an instrument, or some unique project, they dive deep. Encouraging them to share can be a great way to bond, as they feel excited to show what they have made or learned. They might also like to hear your thoughts. Giving honest but kind feedback can spark good conversations. Scorpios often return that support by taking interest in your passions too, creating a healthy exchange of ideas.

A Scorpio friend can be steady over the years, even if life changes. They may not chat every single day, but they keep you in their thoughts. If you reconnect after months of quiet, you might find they still remember your past plans, your family members' names, or small details about your old concerns. This long memory can feel comforting. It shows that their friendship is not just about the moment but about the entire story of who you are. Scorpio's sense of history runs deep, so they might even recall special dates or events that you thought they had forgotten.

CHAPTER 8: SCORPIO AT HOME

When thinking about Scorpio at home, one key idea is comfort mixed with privacy. Many Scorpios see their home as a safe space where they can relax, feel secure, and guard their personal boundaries. They might enjoy having certain areas in the house just for themselves, like a cozy room or a private corner. Even if they share a home with family or roommates, they often want a spot they can call their own. This could be a small reading nook, a home office, or even a corner with soft pillows. Feeling safe and able to step away from outside pressures can be very important to Scorpio.

Scorpios often appreciate a home environment that feels calm yet holds a sense of depth or atmosphere. They might choose colors like deep blue, burgundy, or shades of gray for walls or decorations. Some might add accents of black or dark purple. These choices can create a space that feels intimate and slightly mysterious. Bright lights may not always be their favorite, so they could prefer soft lamps or warm lighting instead of harsh overhead lights. They may use candles or diffused lighting to set a mood. In general, their home might have a peaceful but somewhat dramatic vibe that reflects their inner world.

If a Scorpio is living with parents or siblings, they might spend time in their room more than in common areas. This is not always because they dislike family time, but because they enjoy having a place to think and recharge. Family members might see them as quiet or reserved at home, stepping out for meals or short chats. If the family respects their need for personal space, the Scorpio usually feels more relaxed and can open up when they are ready.

They might join family movie nights or dinners but still prefer to retreat afterwards to read, play games, or do personal projects.

For a Scorpio parent, home can be a place to guide and protect their children. They might be firm about rules that matter, such as honesty and fairness. Scorpio parents might also create routines that feel safe for the family. Their home could reflect their desire for balance: a place where children can explore but also learn respect for boundaries. Sometimes, Scorpio parents might keep parts of their personal life or stress hidden, wanting to maintain a calm environment for the kids. They can be strict if they sense dishonesty, but they are also deeply caring. Their home might feature smaller spaces where the family can bond in cozy surroundings.

In terms of décor, Scorpios might like objects with personal meaning. Rather than filling the home with random knickknacks, they may choose items that hold stories or memories. For instance, a painting that reminds them of a special place, or a shelf of books that reflects their interests. They might also enjoy decorative pieces linked to deep or mysterious themes, like sculptures of mythic creatures or photos of night skies. These items can spark conversation, though a Scorpio may not always share the full story behind them. Part of the home's charm might be that it hints at hidden depths, just like Scorpio themselves.

Privacy can be a high priority. Some Scorpios prefer to keep curtains drawn or choose a house design that does not allow easy views from outside. They might feel uneasy if neighbors can see in too easily. If they have the means, they could invest in sturdy locks or security systems, not because they are paranoid, but because feeling protected helps them relax. They might also create passwords on personal devices and keep important documents well-guarded. It is not unusual for a Scorpio to have a strong lock on their diary or to place their personal letters in a special box.

When Scorpios welcome guests, they might prefer smaller gatherings where they can actually talk to people rather than large parties. A few close friends might be invited over for a cozy dinner or a movie night. The setting might be relaxed, with comfortable seating and possibly dimmer lighting. Scorpio hosts can be attentive, ensuring their guests have food or drinks. But they also like to keep the environment peaceful. If someone becomes too loud or disruptive, Scorpio might feel uneasy. They want a home that stays calm and friendly, without forced chatter or big social pressures.

For a Scorpio living alone, the home can become a strong reflection of their personal style. They might arrange things in a specific way that suits their routines, such as a reading chair near a window or a desk positioned for minimal distractions. They might keep the environment tidy, but not necessarily in a perfect way—rather, everything has its own place. If they enjoy hobbies like painting, they could have a dedicated corner with their supplies. If they like music, they might invest in quality speakers or headphones. The main goal is to create a private world where they can be themselves fully.

Scorpio children at home might need time to do activities alone. They could have strong feelings, so a quiet space helps them handle emotions without being overwhelmed. Parents or siblings might notice that the Scorpio child is not always in the center of play but instead reading or drawing in a private corner. It can help to gently invite them to join group fun, while still respecting their choice. These children may be close to a sibling they trust, sharing secrets that others are not allowed to hear. They may also keep diaries or journals to express thoughts they do not want to say out loud.

One of Scorpio's strong points at home is their willingness to maintain order in areas they care about. They might be the family member who insists on a certain schedule or method to do chores, like washing dishes in a certain order or putting tools back exactly where they belong. This sense of structure can sometimes feel strict to others, but it can also ensure that things stay organized. If other family members respect Scorpio's system, the home can run smoothly. However, if they see it as controlling, conflicts may arise. Communication can help everyone find a balance that works.

Scorpio might also take an interest in cooking, especially if they see it as a private or creative pastime. They might like trying new recipes with deep or rich flavors, such as spicy sauces or dark chocolate desserts. Some Scorpios enjoy cooking for those they love, but they may not want an audience while they work. They might prefer to surprise people with the final result. If they do share the kitchen, they will likely want clear roles: one person chops, another stirs, so they can keep track of each step. The comfort of a home-cooked meal can be a favorite way for Scorpio to express care.

At home, Scorpios might be drawn to music or movies that match their inner depth. They could keep a collection of dramatic films, mystery series, or documentaries about serious topics. When they settle down to watch, they want to fully absorb the story. They might turn off the lights and focus on the screen without chatting. If a family member or roommate talks a lot during the film, they might get annoyed. Quiet, focused viewing can be their way of relaxing. Music can also play a big role in their routine, with genres that reflect strong emotion or have meaningful lyrics.

Home is also where Scorpio can express hidden parts of themselves, possibly through writing, painting, or designing. They might keep a private journal or a sketchbook in a desk drawer. Some Scorpios use these creative outlets to process emotions. They do not always share their creations with others, feeling it is too personal. Having a secure spot in the house for these projects can be very important. If they feel that someone might snoop, they might hide or lock away their supplies. Respecting a Scorpio's privacy in these matters is essential to keeping a peaceful household and keeping trust strong.

Scorpios can be protective over family members in their home. If they sense any danger or threat, they might become very serious about it. This could be as simple as putting up safety measures or teaching children how to handle certain risks. They could also become watchful if they suspect a neighbor or visitor is untrustworthy. While this protectiveness can feel comforting, it can also be intense if Scorpio's suspicions are high. Clear communication helps. If the rest of the family feels safe, Scorpio might need reassurance that everything is fine. Their watchful nature can calm if they see no real harm is present.

Scorpio often invests in quality over quantity. If they buy furniture or home items, they might choose fewer pieces but select them carefully. They might prefer a sturdy wooden table with character rather than a cheaper option that breaks easily. This applies to bedding, kitchen utensils, and even home technology. They would rather save up for something that lasts longer and fits their personal taste. This approach can give their home a comfortable, well-made feel. They might also enjoy antique or secondhand pieces that have a story behind them. Each item they choose can carry meaning beyond just being functional.

In a shared living arrangement, Scorpio may have rules about privacy that everyone must follow. For instance, they might set boundaries such as knocking before entering their room or asking permission before borrowing items. If someone breaks these rules, Scorpio could become upset or distant. They need to know that their personal space and belongings are respected. Conversely, they also try to respect others' areas. They do not want to pry, because they know how important privacy can be. Achieving a respectful balance in the household can help Scorpio feel relaxed and can keep everyone's relationships steady.

Scorpios can have a certain magnetism that shows even at home. Family members or roommates might find themselves drawn to Scorpio's calm presence in the living room. Yet, Scorpio might not talk all the time. Their quiet confidence can make others want to hang around, asking for advice or just enjoying the peaceful atmosphere. Because Scorpio observes more than they speak, they might notice unspoken family dynamics—perhaps a sibling is upset, or a roommate is worried. Scorpio can then step in at the right time, offering a few supportive words. In this way, they become a steady figure at home.

When arguments happen at home, Scorpio can hold onto hurt feelings if the disagreement is serious. They might not explode in rage, but they can become cold or withdrawn. Family or roommates might not even realize how upset they are unless someone asks directly. Over time, if no one addresses the conflict, Scorpio can develop lingering resentment. Having open talks can help them release any bottled-up anger. They might appreciate a calm setting, perhaps in a quiet room where they feel safe expressing themselves. Once they feel heard and respected, they can let go of tension and move toward making peace.

Friends who visit a Scorpio's home might notice personal touches that reflect strong emotional energy. There could be framed photos of loved ones or special moments. Even if the décor looks cool or moody on the surface, there might be warm details hidden around—like a soft blanket or a set of carefully chosen books. Scorpio balances their need for mystery with a desire for comfort. They might place meaningful keepsakes in places they can see each day. A visitor who shows genuine interest in these items may find

Scorpio opening up about personal stories, turning a brief visit into a deeper connection.

Scorpios often value routines at home that help them handle daily life. Waking up and going to bed at set times, scheduling chores, or planning meals can provide a sense of order. This does not mean they are rigid about everything, but they do like to know that certain tasks are done. It lowers stress and gives them more room for the deeper interests they enjoy. If others in the house do not follow these routines, Scorpio might get annoyed. They may speak up about it or try to compromise, but they will likely want some structure to keep the home peaceful.

If a Scorpio owns pets, they often form a strong bond with them. They might choose animals that have a quiet nature or a bit of mystery, such as cats or exotic fish. They take the time to observe their pets' moods and habits, building trust slowly. A Scorpio might enjoy late evenings quietly reading while a cat curls up beside them. Pets can provide calm companionship, letting Scorpio feel less alone without requiring constant interaction. Scorpios usually treat animals with respect, giving them good care and paying attention to their needs. Their protective side might show if a pet looks unwell.

At home, Scorpios may also have personal rituals. They might light incense or candles to create a soothing atmosphere at the end of the day. Some may meditate or do light stretching in a calm corner of the room. Others could keep a gratitude list or read inspiring quotes to maintain emotional balance. These small habits help them manage the intensity of their feelings. They might not discuss these rituals with everyone, seeing them as private methods of self-care. If they live with others, they usually find a time and place where they can follow these routines without interruption.

For technology, a Scorpio in the home might be selective about devices and online presence. They could have strong passwords, rarely leave their phone unlocked, and not share personal photos freely on social media. They might keep their computer organized, with folders named clearly, so they do not lose track of important documents. If someone in the household is careless with shared devices, Scorpio might become concerned about privacy. They believe that what happens at home should stay at home, unless there is a good reason to post or share it. Their care for security can sometimes seem strict, but it helps them feel safer.

Scorpio does not usually enjoy clutter in their personal space. They might have a method for keeping items in order, even if others think the system is unusual. For instance, they might group books by topic rather than alphabetical order, or store belongings in boxes that are labeled by mood or memory. As long as it makes sense to them, that is what matters. If someone else goes in and rearranges things, Scorpio might feel upset because it breaks their sense of control. They want to know exactly where to find each item, so they can relax knowing their private domain is in order.

For relaxation, a Scorpio might enjoy soaking in a warm bath or shower, especially if they live in a place with a comfortable bathroom. Water can help them unwind, matching their status as a water sign. They might light candles or play soft music to enhance the mood. This alone time can help wash away stress from the day. If they share the home, they might take longer than others in the bathroom, making it their mini personal spa. Respecting that need can prevent small disagreements. This ritual can be an important part of how Scorpio maintains emotional well-being at home.

Scorpio's creative side might stand out in their living spaces. They could paint an accent wall with a bold color or design a unique shelf arrangement. Some might make art projects that reflect personal experiences, then hang them on the walls. If they share the house, they may check with others first, but they still want the space to feel like it carries part of their spirit. If they cannot change the home physically, they might set up a digital photo frame or place small decorative items on a shelf. These touches make the home feel like an extension of themselves.

If guests stay overnight, Scorpio usually wants clear boundaries. They can be gracious, offering comfortable sheets, towels, and maybe a snack. But they also expect the guest to respect house rules. They might mention "Lights out by this time," or "Knock before entering my study." These are not meant to be unfriendly. Scorpios simply believe that shared respect keeps everyone comfortable. If a guest ignores these guidelines, Scorpio might not say much immediately, but they will remember. On the other hand, a respectful guest who shows gratitude can earn Scorpio's genuine warmth. The next morning, Scorpio might make breakfast or share a private story.

Scorpios can be very aware of scents at home. They might use scented candles, essential oils, or fragrant plants. Smells like sandalwood, patchouli, or jasmine can create the deep, rich environment they crave. While some might prefer simpler scents, the key is that they notice them. If the house smells musty or unclean, a Scorpio might feel bothered without fully knowing why. They might keep windows open for fresh air if the neighborhood is quiet. Otherwise, they choose subtle ways to keep the home's aroma pleasant. They may also be sensitive to strong chemical smells, preferring natural cleaning products.

In a family setting, Scorpio siblings might share intense bonds. At home, they could compete but also protect each other. If an outsider speaks poorly of their sibling, Scorpio might rush to defend them. However, inside the house, they might argue over small things like borrowed items or noise levels. The relationship can be strong if there is mutual respect. Parents can help by letting Scorpio siblings have private areas. Scorpio's trust grows when they know their siblings will not snoop. Over time, these siblings can become quite close, sharing secrets or inside jokes that no one else in the family understands.

A Scorpio at home may also enjoy reading books on mystery, science, history, or anything that digs beneath the surface. They might keep a stack of these books near their bed or favorite chair. Late at night, they could be found lost in a story. If they share space with others, they hope for quiet, so they can immerse themselves. They might also watch documentaries about deep subjects. The home environment is where Scorpio feels safe to explore these interests fully. If they have a partner or friend who shares this love of learning, they might discuss interesting facts or theories over meals.

If a Scorpio invests in home improvements, they usually do so with a clear goal. They might build a hidden storage space or upgrade a part of the house that improves overall comfort, like better insulation or nicer bedding. They prefer projects that add to the home's coziness or privacy, rather than just following trends. They might also be mindful about security, installing better doors or window locks. While they might not talk a lot about home improvement plans, they can work steadily behind the scenes. Friends or relatives might visit and notice that everything feels more secure and snug than before.

Scorpios may like hosting deep conversations with family members after dinner. They could turn off the TV and ask how everyone's day went, diving into more personal topics. They are not interested in shallow talk. If a family member had a problem, Scorpio might encourage them to share details. This can create a household culture where people open up. However, if others are not used to being so honest, it might feel awkward. Scorpio should try not to push too hard. Allowing each person to speak or stay quiet as they prefer keeps the atmosphere peaceful. Over time, such talks can become bonding moments.

Scorpio children might keep meaningful objects in a special box under their bed or in a drawer. They store letters from friends, shells from the beach, or small trinkets that hold emotional value. Parents might find that the child is protective of these items and does not want them moved or touched. It is wise to respect this. The Scorpio child's sense of ownership over personal memories is strong. They might also rearrange these treasures from time to time, reflecting on old times. This habit can continue into adulthood, leading to a Scorpio who cherishes keepsakes that remind them of the past.

If a Scorpio is renting a place, they often still personalize it as much as possible. They might not be allowed to paint walls, but they will add unique furniture or wall hangings. They will organize their closet carefully to maintain order. If house rules are strict, Scorpio might silently follow them, but they will carve out a private corner. Having a place to think and recharge is very important. They might also build strong relationships with neighbors if the neighbors seem respectful. But they do not usually share personal details freely. Trust grows slowly, even if they see each other often.

In a romantic partnership, Scorpio may invite their partner into a special area of the home once they feel comfortable. Maybe they set up a reading corner with a soft blanket, a candle, and a seat for two. Sharing this space can be a big step, signaling that they feel safe enough to let their partner see their more private world. If the partner respects boundaries, Scorpio might open up even more, talking about their dreams or worries. The home can become a place of close connection, where Scorpio's deeper feelings can be discussed without fear of judgment.

Some Scorpios might like to keep a small garden or a few houseplants at home. Though they are a water sign, they can enjoy caring for living things, watching them grow silently. They may pick plants that do not demand too much bright sunlight or constant watering, matching their preference for a somewhat subdued environment. They watch the leaves for signs of health and might research ways to help their plants thrive. This gentle activity can be calming, giving them a sense of connection to nature. If space allows, they might grow herbs for cooking or have a cozy corner with larger green plants.

When Scorpio is tired from work or school, they might come home and immediately want quiet. If they share the house with others, they could greet everyone briefly, then go to their room to recharge. This does not mean they are angry or ignoring anyone. It just means they need a bit of silence to let go of the day's stress. After some downtime, they can emerge feeling more at ease. Family members who understand this pattern can avoid pushing Scorpio to join activities right away. By giving them a moment to relax, they can share calmer, happier moments later.

If Scorpio has housemates who enjoy loud gatherings, there can be friction. Scorpio might not like frequent parties or random guests, especially if it disrupts their sense of security. They might try to compromise by setting specific rules about quiet hours or giving a heads-up when guests will visit. If housemates do not respect these wishes, Scorpio could look for a new living arrangement. Feeling safe at home is essential to them. They may also explore ways to soundproof their room or invest in noise-canceling headphones. Finding a good balance is important, since Scorpio's well-being depends on having a place to decompress.

Scorpios usually do not share every aspect of their day with family or roommates. Even if they had an eventful afternoon, they might talk about it only if asked directly. They might think, "If you want to know, you'll ask." Some family members could mistake this for disinterest, but it is simply Scorpio's style. If someone is curious, they can ask, "How was your day?" and Scorpio will likely open up. They do not always volunteer information. Similarly, if the family environment is too pushy, Scorpio might become tight-lipped. A relaxed approach invites them to share more naturally.

Scorpio tends to keep personal records at home in a neat way, whether it is bills, important documents, or diaries. They might have folders labeled by category or date. They feel more at peace knowing they can find what they need quickly. If a friend or partner rummages through their things, they might react strongly. These papers or files could contain personal thoughts or plans. Scorpio does not like anyone reading them without permission. This protective stance can extend to digital data too. Passwords and locked files help them manage who sees what. In their view, privacy in the home is vital for emotional health.

In parent-child relationships, a Scorpio child might respect parents who give them a chance to explore their feelings without intrusion. The child could have days when they come home from school upset but say nothing. A gentle question like, "Would you like to talk about anything?" might work better than demanding, "Tell me now!" Over time, as trust builds, the child might reveal more. The home environment shapes how Scorpio children learn to express or hide emotions. If the atmosphere is supportive and calm, they can develop healthy habits. If it is tense or controlling, they might shut down and refuse to share.

For extended family gatherings, a Scorpio at home might prefer to have a plan. They could be anxious about too many relatives crowding the space. Knowing which rooms are set up for guests and which areas remain private can help them feel in control. They might decorate the living room nicely but keep their own bedroom off-limits. If they trust certain relatives, they may allow them a brief peek at personal collections or rooms, then gently steer them back to common areas. Maintaining this boundary helps Scorpio stay comfortable during gatherings that can otherwise feel overwhelming.

Scorpio's approach to chores at home might be steady and thorough. If it is their turn to clean the kitchen, they might do it carefully, wiping counters and rearranging items in a tidy manner. They do not love random or rushed work. If others in the house do a careless job, Scorpio might feel frustrated. Sometimes, they might simply redo it themselves to ensure it is done right. They could speak up, hoping to establish clear standards so that everyone shares the effort fairly. If they see a housemate stepping up responsibly, Scorpio will appreciate it and likely express thanks in their own reserved way.

A Scorpio at home often finds comfort in small daily rituals. This might include lighting a scented candle each evening, brewing a cup of herbal tea, or sitting by a window to watch the sky for a few minutes. These little habits calm their mind and let them reflect on the day. In a busy household, they might schedule these moments when they will not be disturbed, such as late at night or early in the morning. Over time, these regular habits become a protective shield against stress. They can be a silent promise to themselves: no matter how chaotic life gets, home is where they can find calm.

Managing anger or worry at home can be easier for Scorpio if they have a private spot to release tension. Some might keep a punching bag in the garage, while others might scribble in a journal. They may also listen to intense music or watch a film that mirrors their mood, finding a way to channel strong emotions. If they have supportive roommates or family, a gentle knock on Scorpio's door saying, "I'm here if you need to talk," can help. But forcing them to share can backfire. They usually want to speak when they are ready, on their own terms.

Scorpios might also be in tune with the home's energy. They notice if tensions are rising, even if no one has said anything. They might see that one sibling is avoiding another or that a parent is worried about money. While they do not always confront these issues directly, they carry an inner awareness. If a problem persists, they could approach someone privately, asking if everything is all right. They like to fix problems at the root. However, if the household is chaotic and no one wants to address issues, Scorpio might withdraw to protect their own peace, feeling powerless to change the overall mood.

Holidays or special days at home can show Scorpio's quieter approach to togetherness. They might not be the type to decorate every inch of the house with flashy items, but they could place a few meaningful decorations. For instance, a handmade ornament or a wreath with darker tones. They may prefer small gatherings with close family instead of hosting big neighborhood events. They enjoy the depth of personal connection more than the noise of large crowds. If they do celebrate with a bigger group, they might slip away now and then to breathe. Returning to a calm corner helps them manage the social energy.

Scorpios can also find joy in investigating the history of the place they live. They might look up past owners of their home or local legends if it is an older building. This can add an extra layer of meaning. Some might collect stories about the area, enjoying the sense of mystery. If they find out something interesting, they might only share it with family or close friends, seeing it as a personal treasure. This reflects Scorpio's love for hidden truths and deeper understanding. Their home thus becomes more than just a building—it holds a story that resonates with their inquisitive mind.

Overall, Scorpio wants a home that feels like a true sanctuary. This extends beyond physical safety. They want emotional security, too. If they live with family, a partner, or roommates, open respect is essential. Clear boundaries, honest communication, and acceptance of each other's personal space help Scorpio feel at ease. In return, Scorpio's devotion to the home environment can bring stability and depth. They might offer a listening ear when someone is upset or keep important routines that benefit everyone. Their presence can be a steady anchor, provided their privacy is upheld and their emotional side is acknowledged.

In the end, Scorpio at home is a blend of coziness and quiet power. They shape their living space to reflect their tastes—often rich colors, meaningful items, and calming lighting. Whether living alone or with others, they strive for privacy, emotional safety, and a sense of order. By respecting Scorpio's boundaries and giving them freedom to recharge, loved ones can share a warm connection in that space. This sign's watchful, caring side can support the household, while their need for introspection helps them process life's ups and downs. The home becomes a nest of calm, loyalty, and honesty, deeply echoing Scorpio's true nature.

CHAPTER 9: SCORPIO AT WORK

When thinking about Scorpio at work, it helps to remember that they bring a strong sense of focus to whatever tasks they handle. They tend to be goal-driven and like to see progress. A Scorpio might prefer jobs or roles that allow them to go deep into a topic, solving problems or analyzing details. Because of their water-sign nature, they can sense hidden issues. In a busy office, they might observe how people behave before they speak up. This watchful approach can help them spot what needs fixing. They do not always rush to share their ideas, but once they do, they often present them with confidence.

Scorpio's calm exterior can be an advantage in stressful workplaces. While others might panic about a tight deadline, Scorpio often keeps a level head. They might still feel pressure inside, but they try not to show it. This allows them to concentrate on what must be done. Colleagues might see Scorpio as steady in a crisis, able to handle a large workload without complaining loudly. Sometimes, they tackle tasks in a quiet, focused way that surprises others when the results appear. Scorpio's determination can help them push through challenges that might discourage people who do not have such a firm mindset.

In many work environments, Scorpio likes clear responsibilities. They want to understand exactly what they must do to succeed. If the job is too vague, they might become frustrated or uncertain. Giving Scorpio a defined task or project can help them excel. They will likely approach it step by step, looking for hidden problems to fix or better methods to use. If they spot inefficiencies, they might take notes privately, then offer a plan to address these issues. Some coworkers might be surprised by how detailed Scorpio's plan is, but it comes from the sign's deep thinking and focus on improvement.

Teamwork can be interesting for Scorpios. They often prefer to handle their portion of a project on their own, so they can control the quality and manage the details. However, they do recognize the value of working with others. If the team is organized and fair, Scorpio might enjoy sharing ideas and dividing tasks. But if they see laziness or dishonesty, they can become frustrated. They do not like seeing people skate by without effort. They also dislike gossip or drama in the office. If a team project has such issues, Scorpio may withdraw and just focus on their own part, trying to avoid conflict.

Leadership roles can fit Scorpio well if they feel prepared. They might not always crave the spotlight, but they can rise to leadership by showing a steady hand and thorough knowledge. Once in charge, they usually run a tight ship. They set rules clearly and expect everyone to follow them. They might also assign tasks based on each person's strengths, using their skill at reading people. However, a Scorpio boss can seem strict if employees are not used to direct feedback. They often point out mistakes plainly, though not necessarily in a mean way. Their main goal is to keep projects on track and ensure quality results.

Scorpios can handle confidential information with care. If the job involves private data or secret plans, they are often good choices to keep these matters safe. They understand the importance of trust and do not want to betray the company or clients. This can make them excellent in roles like research, investigation, strategy, or any field where sensitive details must be protected. They typically follow the rules about privacy and may even propose stricter security measures if they see a risk. Their natural tendency to keep quiet can be an asset, helping them guard details until it is time to share them with the right people.

Because Scorpios are observant, they might pick up on office politics quickly. They see who has influence, which groups form alliances, and who might be hiding negative motives. This can help them avoid pitfalls at work. If a coworker tries to spread rumors, Scorpio often senses something is off. They may not confront the person publicly, but they keep a mental note. If they trust a colleague, they might quietly warn them to watch out. Over time, Scorpio can build a reputation as someone who is wise about workplace dynamics. However, they only share these insights with people they genuinely trust.

Scorpio can be quite driven by success. They like to set high standards for their own performance. Some may aim for promotions or recognition, but they do not always talk about it. Instead, they let their work speak. Others might not realize how determined Scorpio is until they see how consistently they deliver. This persistent drive can lead them to climb the career ladder. However, Scorpios might clash with supervisors if they feel the rules are unfair. They do not enjoy pointless tasks or micromanagement. If a boss tries to control every detail, Scorpio may feel trapped, which can lower their motivation.

Handling feedback at work can be tricky for Scorpio. They appreciate honest feedback when it is clear and helpful. But if it feels unfair or overly harsh, they might take it to heart and brood about it. Because they are proud of their work, they want any criticism to be balanced by specific advice on how to improve. If they sense a boss or coworker is picking on them for personal reasons, they can become resentful. On the other hand, if the feedback is sincere and meant to help, Scorpio can accept it and use it to get better at what they do.

Scorpios might also be protective of colleagues they respect. If they see a teammate being bullied or blamed unfairly, they can step in with calm but firm support. They believe in loyalty, so if they have formed a bond with someone, they will defend that person. This loyalty can earn them close friendships at work. But if they feel a coworker has broken their trust, they might distance themselves. They dislike backstabbing or secret plots. A Scorpio who senses betrayal in the workplace can become cold or even look for ways to shield themselves from future harm. Trust is key to their feeling at ease among coworkers.

In certain roles, Scorpios thrive because of their ability to concentrate deeply. Fields like research, forensics, psychology, science, engineering, or finance might appeal to them. They can dig into complex data or problems without getting bored. Their curiosity pushes them to learn more and figure out how things work. If the job requires secrecy or security, Scorpio's natural sense of caution comes in handy. They also do well in roles where they can bring about real change, such as crisis management or positions that let them fix underlying issues. This drive to uncover hidden layers can make them standout problem solvers.

At times, Scorpio may prefer working in a quieter environment, where they can think and focus. Open-plan offices with constant noise or random chatter might drain them. They can still do well there if they have noise-canceling headphones or a small corner to retreat to. But ideally, they like a space where they can control distractions. Some Scorpios even choose to work alone or start their own businesses for that reason. Working from home can also be an attractive option if it gives them the privacy they crave. By shaping a calmer workspace, Scorpio can tap into their full potential and remain productive.

In group discussions or meetings, Scorpio may not always be the first to speak. They want to hear others' views and gather facts. Then, they might offer a well-thought-out statement that addresses the core issue. Coworkers might notice that when Scorpio does speak, it carries weight because it is so deliberate. This can help the team see new angles or consider problems more carefully. However, if a meeting is too chaotic, Scorpio could shut down, preferring to share thoughts later in a smaller setting or by email. They value clarity over messy, fast-paced arguments where no one listens well.

Scorpios can be good mentors if they decide to guide a younger or less experienced coworker. They might share knowledge privately, giving tips based on real insights. They do not enjoy bragging, so they likely will not announce this mentorship to the whole company. Instead, they quietly show the ropes. If the person they help proves loyal and hardworking, Scorpio might develop a lasting professional connection with them. But if they sense laziness or disloyalty, they will stop investing time in that person. Their approach to mentoring reflects their overall style: they give energy to relationships that feel genuine and respectful.

On the subject of honesty at work, Scorpio values truth but also knows that not all information must be shared openly. They can keep strategic plans or sensitive details under wraps if it benefits the team or company. However, they draw a line at telling lies or deceiving others for personal gain. If they see a manager lying to customers or cheating the system, they may feel torn. They dislike unethical behavior and might eventually speak up or leave for a more honest workplace. They prefer to stay in a job where they do not have to betray their own sense of integrity.

One of Scorpio's big strengths at work is their ability to notice patterns or hidden gaps. They might look at sales numbers and spot a trend no one else saw. They could read customer feedback and realize the real problem is not what people think. With their detective-like mind, Scorpios can excel at solving puzzles or digging into big data. This skill can put them in positions where they investigate or audit processes, making sure everything lines up. Other employees might appreciate how Scorpio can find the root cause of a recurring problem, allowing the team to fix it for good.

Scorpios also keep an eye on their own reputation at work. They may not chase constant praise, but they do care about how they are perceived. If they realize someone is spreading rumors, they might handle it quietly, possibly talking one-on-one with that person or gathering evidence to clear their name. They tend to avoid dramatic confrontations unless they see no other option. Yet, they will stand up for themselves if needed. If they sense real harm, they could gather proof to protect their position. This cautious approach means they do not ignore threats, but they also do not waste energy on minor gossip.

When it comes to deadlines, Scorpios typically prefer having enough time to do things thoroughly. They do not like rushing through projects because they fear missing details. If forced to work under a very tight schedule, they can still manage, but they might feel stressed. Their sense of perfection can make them anxious if they believe they cannot reach the standard they want. However, they usually rise to the challenge, even if it means staying late or working extra hard. Coworkers might see them as dedicated and determined, but also possibly too serious about small points. For Scorpio, quality matters a lot.

In a manager's view, a Scorpio employee can be seen as reliable and thorough. They will likely complete tasks well and keep confidential matters safe. If a supervisor praises them in front of the team, Scorpio might accept it quietly but not make a big show of gratitude. Their pride is more private. If the manager scolds them wrongly, they can become resentful or distant. Communication with Scorpio works best when it is based on facts and respect. Telling them exactly what was done right or wrong is better than being vague. They want to know how to improve without feeling attacked.

Networking events can be challenging for Scorpio, who might not enjoy small talk with many strangers. They can handle it if they see real value in meeting key people or learning important details. Still, they prefer meaningful conversations to random chatter. If forced into a big gathering, they might seek out a quiet corner or chat with one or two individuals who seem honest and interesting. They do not want to waste time with those who only boast about themselves. Instead, they look for people who share serious goals or have insights to exchange. This approach can lead to fewer but stronger work connections.

Scorpio may also be skilled at negotiation or bargaining, especially if they have prepared. They do not mind waiting out the other side, watching for weaknesses. Their calm can be intimidating, because they do not show panic or hurry. This can prove useful in business deals or conflict resolution. If they sense the other person is bluffing, they might remain silent until the real offer emerges. Scorpio's thorough research helps them walk into these situations with facts. They are less likely to be tricked by fancy words. Instead, they trust evidence and gut feelings, combining logic with their natural intuition.

Self-motivation is often high for Scorpio, but they can lose interest if the work feels pointless. They want to see progress, or at least a reason behind each task. If a project seems meaningless, they may do it but with less energy. They prefer roles that offer challenges, letting them develop new skills or uncover better ways to work. Sometimes, they can be found in positions with growth potential or in places where they can specialize. If the job becomes stale, Scorpio might quietly start searching for a new opportunity. They rarely make a big fuss, preferring a controlled transition if possible.

A Scorpio might keep a neat or at least well-structured workspace. Whether it is a desk in an office or a corner at home, they like to have files, notes, and tools organized. They might set up folders labeled by topic or date. They might even have a personal system for labeling. While it may look simple on the surface, it contains enough detail to help them find things easily. They do not want coworkers rummaging through their desk without asking, because they value privacy. If someone does so, Scorpio can become upset. They see their workspace as both a reflection of themselves and a safe zone.

When dealing with clients, Scorpio can come across as calm and trustworthy. They do not tend to overpromise or use flashy words. Instead, they speak with quiet confidence, explaining the facts and potential outcomes. Clients may sense that Scorpio is not trying to trick them. This can build strong long-term relationships. If the client is difficult, Scorpio might use careful listening to find the real cause of the problem. They can handle complaints with patience, though if the client is rude or dishonest, Scorpio's patience might wear thin. Still, they remain professional, focusing on solutions. That calm approach helps diffuse tense situations.

A common struggle for Scorpio is balancing their strong drive with rest. They might work long hours if they feel they must. Over time, this can lead to burnout. Scorpios often refuse to show weakness, so they keep pushing themselves. Coworkers might not realize how tired or stressed Scorpio is, because outwardly they seem fine. To avoid burnout, Scorpios benefit from small breaks or short walks to clear the mind. They can also learn to delegate tasks if they are in a leadership role. By sharing the load, they avoid reaching a point where their productivity drops due to exhaustion.

In creative fields, Scorpio's depth can shine. Artists, writers, designers, or performers who are Scorpio might explore intense themes in their work. They are not afraid to tackle subjects that others find heavy or complex. This can set them apart, earning them a reputation for meaningful projects. They might pour personal feelings or experiences into their art, resulting in powerful creations. In such environments, Scorpio can be both introverted and expressive, using their craft to share deeper truths. Coworkers in creative teams might be impressed by how Scorpio channels strong emotion into designs, scripts, or performances that leave a lasting impact.

Scorpios are not always fans of group brainstorming sessions that lack structure. While others might throw out random ideas, Scorpio may sit quietly, waiting for a plan. If the meeting seems scattered, they might lose patience. A better approach is to let Scorpio prepare before the session, thinking about ideas on their own first. Then they can bring solid suggestions to the table. If the group respects this method, Scorpio can contribute valuable insights. They dislike feeling pressured to come up with instant answers without time to reflect. Giving them a bit of space to think can lead to more thoughtful input.

A Scorpio's relationship with authority depends on whether they respect the person in charge. If they see strong leadership skills, honesty, and fairness, they can become loyal supporters. But if the boss is weak, unfair, or deceptive, Scorpio may have a hard time following them. They might comply outwardly, but inside they question every decision. In extreme cases, they could look for another job. They do not want to stay where they cannot trust leadership. Because they value integrity, a bad manager can push Scorpio away. On the flip side, a good manager who fosters trust might find Scorpio to be a dedicated and productive team member.

Setting boundaries at work is important to Scorpio. They do not like coworkers prying into their personal life. If someone tries to force personal questions, Scorpio might give a polite but vague answer. They separate their professional role from who they are outside of work. Over time, they may open up if a coworker becomes a real friend. However, they do not want the entire office to know every detail about their private world. This boundary helps them stay focused on tasks and avoid unnecessary drama. Colleagues might call them "mysterious," but Scorpio prefers that over feeling exposed in a public setting.

Technology is another area where Scorpio can excel, especially if it requires careful data analysis or security knowledge. They might enjoy coding, database management, or cybersecurity roles. Their ability to spot patterns and keep secrets safe suits these fields. They might also prefer handling back-end work rather than front-end tasks that require constant public interaction. If the job allows them to explore hidden layers of code or solve tough tech issues, they can become deeply engaged. This suits their nature as investigators who want to know how things operate. Their attention to detail can prevent mistakes that could cause big problems later.

Scorpio's communication style at work can sometimes be short and to the point. They do not like wasting time with fluff. Emails or messages they send might be direct, focusing on the main idea. Some coworkers appreciate the clarity, while others might prefer more polite small talk. Scorpio tries to remain courteous but might not add lots of extras. If they feel they need to clarify, they will, but they do not tend to write long, flowery paragraphs. This no-nonsense approach can help them avoid confusion, though it can also make them seem distant or cold to those who expect more friendly chatter.

Handling office friendships requires care. Scorpio can form tight bonds with a few coworkers they respect and trust. They might share personal jokes or help each other with tasks. However, they keep the circle small. They do not want to be seen as part of a gossip group or as someone who shares company secrets. If another coworker tries to fish for private info, Scorpio might politely sidestep. They guard friendships the same way they guard personal life details. Once they choose a friend at work, they often stand by them. But if that friend betrays them, Scorpio might quietly end the bond and stay professional instead.

In conflict situations, Scorpio tries not to start fights, but they will defend themselves or their work if attacked. They can remain calm on the surface, which might unnerve the other person. Scorpio often prefers a private discussion instead of a public showdown. They gather facts, present their side, and watch the reaction. If the conflict is not resolved, they might go up the chain of command or document everything for protection. They believe in standing firm for what is right, but they dislike public scenes. If the workplace has constant drama, Scorpio may eventually look for a quieter environment that allows them to focus on actual tasks.

Scorpio's ability to keep secrets can lead coworkers to confide in them. They might become aware of personal struggles or doubts that others face. While Scorpio can offer a kind ear, they also worry about getting entangled in messy politics. If a coworker shares sensitive news, Scorpio might offer advice in a private setting, urging them to handle it properly. They do not want to be a gossip source. If the matter is truly serious, they might suggest talking to a supervisor or human resources. Scorpio's caring side shows in these moments, but they also maintain firm boundaries to avoid trouble.

When giving presentations, Scorpio might speak in a measured, controlled way. They are not usually the loudest or most dramatic speaker, but they tend to be clear and factual. They might use slides or data to back up each point. Because they prefer thorough preparation, they often plan the talk carefully. If someone interrupts with questions, Scorpio answers calmly, unless the question seems disrespectful. Then, they might become more guarded. Coworkers may respect them for providing real substance instead of fluff. Scorpio's depth of knowledge can shine during these moments, showing they understand the project inside and out.

Money matters at work can be important to Scorpio. They value fair pay for effort. If they believe they are underpaid or overlooked, they might gather data about average salaries in their field. They will not make a big scene, but they might request a private meeting to discuss a raise. They approach negotiations with facts, explaining their contributions. If the employer refuses without good reasons, Scorpio could start looking elsewhere. They do not want to waste energy where they are not appreciated. At the same time, they do not demand more than they deserve. They want balance and respect in financial dealings.

Work-life balance can be a challenge for Scorpio. Because they can be so focused on tasks, they sometimes bring work home in their mind. They might replay a conversation or keep thinking about a puzzle they have not solved. Family or roommates could notice Scorpio's mind drifting during dinner. It helps if Scorpio sets boundaries, such as not checking work emails after a certain time or scheduling activities that relax them. Otherwise, their mind might never truly rest. When they do manage to unplug, they can recharge and come back stronger. This can make them more efficient and less prone to burnout over the long term.

Traveling for work might appeal to some Scorpios, especially if it allows them to explore new places without losing privacy. They might be okay with short business trips where they can meet clients or gather data, then return home. If travel becomes constant or chaotic, they could become unhappy. They prefer some stability. If they do travel, they often plan carefully, checking itineraries and local details. They might not join big social outings after meetings, choosing instead to rest in their hotel or explore quietly. This approach helps them handle work travel without feeling drained by too much forced socializing.

Scorpio can excel in crisis management. If a company faces a tough moment—a sudden problem, an unhappy client, or a public misunderstanding—Scorpio can remain level-headed. They quickly analyze the situation, gathering facts. Then they propose a path forward. If others are panicking, Scorpio's steadiness can be a real asset. After the crisis passes, they might reflect on what caused it and how to prevent future issues. They do not just want a bandage fix. They aim to tackle the source of the problem. This approach can earn them respect as someone who handles high-pressure moments without losing their composure.

In a creative team, Scorpio might contribute intense ideas or help refine the group's concepts. They might push for greater depth in marketing campaigns or suggest real stories that tap into strong feelings. Some coworkers appreciate this, while others might find it too serious. Scorpio's style might lead to powerful, memorable results, but it can clash with those who prefer light, easy content. If the team values variety, Scorpio's darker or more profound angle can balance someone else's bright approach. This can create a well-rounded final product. Still, Scorpio must watch that they do not dismiss simpler ideas that also work.

In a customer-facing role, Scorpio might appear calm and collected, which can build trust. They do not usually push for sales with flashy talk. Instead, they present the facts, address concerns, and let the customer decide. This honest method can lead to loyal repeat clients who trust Scorpio's word. However, Scorpio might become frustrated if management pressures them to exaggerate claims or oversell. They value truth in work dealings. If they are forced to do something against their principles, they might quietly rebel or seek a job where they can stay true to their ethics. Maintaining moral comfort is vital for Scorpio's peace of mind.

Scorpio is not always comfortable with office parties or social events. They might attend to show respect or because it could help their career, but they rarely are the life of the party. Instead, they might chat with a small group of people they know well. If the event becomes too loud or superficial, Scorpio could leave early. They prefer deeper one-on-one connections over big crowds. Coworkers might notice that Scorpio vanishes once the event becomes too rowdy. This does not mean Scorpio hates everyone; it is just their way of keeping emotional energy balanced and avoiding too much forced interaction.

When it comes to recognition, Scorpio may appreciate a quiet "thank you" or an official note in their record more than a big public display. They do not typically seek a lot of applause. They want to know their efforts matter, but they feel uneasy if put on stage for show. A sincere award or chance to work on an even bigger project might mean more to them than a big round of applause. Their sense of achievement is often personal: they know they did the job well. Public praise can be nice, but it is not what drives them day to day.

Keeping emotions balanced at work is important. Scorpios might feel intense frustration if a coworker acts unfairly or if a project is blocked by stubborn rules. They often store these feelings inside, then vent them in private. This can be healthy if they have a good outlet, like writing in a journal or talking to a trusted confidant outside the office. However, if they bottle up too much anger, they risk snapping at someone unexpectedly. Learning to address smaller issues early can prevent bigger blowups. Scorpios who find constructive ways to share concerns can keep the work environment calmer for themselves and everyone else.

Scorpios can excel at research-based roles. They like collecting facts, reading through documents, and piecing together clues. They might be the person who compiles reports that others find tedious. Because of their patience, they often spot hidden trends. This can be especially useful in fields like law, market research, or academic studies. They do not mind spending hours verifying data to make sure it is correct. Some might find that dull, but Scorpio sees it as a puzzle to solve. Their final reports often impress managers or teachers because they dig deeper than surface-level facts, revealing insights that others overlook.

Workplace relationships with other zodiac signs can vary. With fire signs, Scorpio might clash if the atmosphere is too rushed or if big talk overshadows detail. With earth signs, Scorpio might form a stable team, since both like reliability and real results. With air signs, Scorpio may feel that everything is too theoretical, but they can learn from fresh ideas. With fellow water signs, emotional understanding can be high, but it might lead to intense discussions. In any case, Scorpio tries to find common ground when possible, focusing on shared goals. They do best in an environment that respects their quiet strength and thorough methods.

When starting a new job, Scorpio usually watches how things work before getting too involved in office chatter. They might quietly learn who does what, how people interact, and what the real chain of command is. This observation helps them avoid stepping on toes or trusting the wrong person too early. Once they feel more comfortable, they begin sharing ideas or suggestions. Coworkers might not even realize Scorpio was studying everything from day one. This approach might seem slow, but it prevents them from making false assumptions. Over time, they build a solid foundation of knowledge that supports their future actions.

In remote or freelance work, Scorpio enjoys the freedom to set their schedule and environment. They can arrange their workspace at home to block out distractions. This can boost their productivity. They also appreciate not having to make small talk daily. However, remote work can be lonely if they do not stay connected with the team. Scorpios may need to schedule calls or occasional meetups to maintain professional relationships. They will still be selective about how much they share, but regular communication can prevent them from feeling isolated. Overall, they can thrive in flexible work setups that respect their need for independence.

Scorpios often keep personal issues separate from work. If they face a tough time at home, they might come to the office and still perform well, hiding any sadness or worry. This can be good for productivity but might lead coworkers to think Scorpio has no problems. In reality, they just prefer not to mix personal life with professional duties. If they ever open up about difficulties, it might be to a single coworker they trust completely. Others might never know. This boundary helps them stay focused on tasks, but it can also create the image that Scorpio is distant or hard to read.

CHAPTER 10: SCORPIO & LOVE

Scorpio and love can be a powerful mix. This sign is known for strong feelings, and that includes matters of the heart. Scorpios do not usually enter relationships lightly. They may act cautiously at first, observing a potential partner to see if they can trust them. Once Scorpio decides to open their heart, the intensity can grow quickly. Their affection tends to be deep, and they often expect real commitment in return. Many people find Scorpio's devotion attractive, but it also comes with high expectations. Loyalty, honesty, and real emotional connection matter greatly to Scorpio when it comes to love.

In the early stages of romance, Scorpios can appear somewhat mysterious. They might not share everything about themselves right away. Instead, they ask questions to learn about the other person. They watch how someone behaves in different situations—small gestures, choice of words, and how they treat others. If something feels off, Scorpio may step back, unsure if they can trust the person. On the other hand, if they see consistent kindness and honesty, they open up more. This slow unveiling of Scorpio's deeper side can draw in partners who enjoy discovering layers in a relationship. It can also frustrate those who prefer quick closeness.

Once a Scorpio decides they truly care about someone, they can be very loyal. They want to protect and support their partner through good times and bad. This does not mean they will ignore problems, though. If they suspect dishonesty, they may become distant or jealous. Jealousy is a common issue for Scorpios in love. They feel things strongly and can worry about losing the person they value. Open communication can help, but if the partner tries to hide things, Scorpio's suspicion can grow. Balancing trust and reassurance becomes important, especially in the early stages of building a lasting bond.

Scorpio might bring a sense of intensity to love that some people find overwhelming. They do not like small or casual commitments. They want a partner who is willing to share deep thoughts, real feelings, and future plans. If a partner is not ready for this depth, disagreements can arise. However, for someone who craves a strong emotional connection, being with Scorpio can feel like finally meeting a partner who truly cares. Scorpios often give their all in a relationship, expecting a similar level of devotion in return. This can lead to passionate love, but also to disappointment if the partner does not match their energy.

In terms of communication, Scorpio in love may choose words carefully. They are not usually the type to flatter or speak sweetly just for show. When they say "I love you," they mean it with all their heart. They might also speak directly about issues, which can seem harsh to a partner who prefers gentle talk. Scorpio believes honesty is key to solving problems, even if it stings at first. This direct style can help couples address misunderstandings quickly. Yet, it also requires both people to remain calm and not take every word too personally. Scorpio does not aim to hurt feelings; they just value truth.

Physical affection can be very important to Scorpio. They often express love through touch, hugs, or other forms of closeness. This does not mean they are clingy in public, but they enjoy an intimate bond in private. If their partner is distant or uninterested in physical contact, Scorpio might worry something is wrong. This sign often sees physical and emotional closeness as linked. They feel safer when they can show love in ways that involve both heart and body. Partners who understand this can find Scorpio's affectionate side quite comforting. Those who see it as too intense may need to talk about boundaries early on.

Scorpios can be protective in love. If they sense anyone threatening or harming their partner, they can stand up fiercely. This might be a rude coworker, a troublesome ex, or a relative who causes tension. Scorpio is not afraid to speak out if they believe it will help keep their partner safe. On the flip side, a Scorpio might go too far if they let jealousy mix with protectiveness. For example, they could become suspicious of normal friendships. A balanced Scorpio learns to trust their partner's judgment while still being ready to defend them when truly necessary. Striking that balance can strengthen the relationship.

When it comes to conflict, Scorpio may hold onto hurt feelings for a while, especially if they feel betrayed. They might not scream or shout, but they can become cold or withdrawn. This can leave a partner feeling shut out, uncertain of how to fix the situation. Talking things through calmly and sincerely is often the best way forward. Scorpio wants to see real regret if they have been wronged, along with clear steps to prevent the issue from happening again. A simple apology might not be enough. They need to feel that their partner respects their trust and does not plan to repeat hurtful actions.

Scorpios can be secretive about certain aspects of their personal life, even with a loved one. This does not always mean they hide major secrets. Sometimes, it is just how they keep control over their emotional space. A partner might notice that Scorpio avoids sharing details of a past heartbreak or family problems right away. Over time, if the partner proves trustworthy, Scorpio may open up. However, if the partner pushes too hard or snoops, Scorpio can feel violated. Patience is key. When Scorpio is ready, they will offer deeper glimpses of their inner world, which can bring the couple closer.

Romantic gestures from Scorpio may be quiet but meaningful. They might remember a favorite dessert or a special song and use it to create a private moment for their partner. They can surprise their loved one with thoughtful gifts that reflect shared memories. This sign tends to pay attention to small details in a partner's likes and dislikes. While they might not plan huge, flashy dates, they aim to make each meeting or celebration personal. Over time, these small but intimate gestures can build a sense of closeness that feels unique to Scorpio's style. Partners often appreciate feeling truly seen and understood.

Scorpio's idea of love often includes emotional honesty. They can sense when a partner is hiding sorrow, anger, or worry. This can be both a blessing and a challenge. On one hand, it helps them care for their partner's needs. On the other hand, they may become frustrated if the partner refuses to open up. A good approach is to talk about feelings before they become too large to handle. Scorpio tries to do the same, although they sometimes keep their own worries inside. If both partners practice honest sharing, it can deepen the bond and prevent serious misunderstandings from festering.

Trust is the foundation of Scorpio's relationships. They do not give it freely, but once it is established, they do not want anything to break it. A single act of disloyalty can cause deep cracks in the bond. Even small lies can raise big questions for Scorpio. Rebuilding trust after a betrayal can take time, with Scorpio needing repeated proof that the partner has changed or truly regrets the mistake. Some Scorpios might choose to end the relationship rather than face the fear of being hurt again. Others may try to work through it, but it requires sincere effort from both sides.

Some Scorpios love to talk about deep topics with their partner—life goals, childhood memories, personal fears, and more. Light chit-chat might feel boring to them in a romantic setting. They want to know their partner's mind and soul. This can create strong intimacy if both sides are comfortable with serious conversations. Partners who prefer to keep things relaxed might feel Scorpio is probing too much. Setting a pace that feels right for both is important. Scorpio should remember that not everyone is ready to share every thought quickly. Respect and gentle pacing help the relationship blossom at a rate both can handle.

When courting or dating, Scorpio might test a partner's sincerity by watching how they handle small challenges. It could be observing how they treat a server at a restaurant or how they respond to a minor disagreement. Scorpio does not always do this on purpose; they simply notice everything. If they see kindness and patience, they feel safer. If they see rudeness or quick temper, they might second-guess the potential for a long-term bond. These "tests" are Scorpio's way of making sure they do not invest love in someone who might hurt them. Over time, if all seems good, Scorpio grows more relaxed and trusting.

Scorpio's passion often extends to long-term partnerships or marriage. They typically do not choose a life partner casually. Many Scorpios think deeply about what marriage or serious commitment means. They might plan for shared finances, living arrangements, and future dreams. In such a bond, they offer unwavering support, expecting the partner to do the same. If children enter the picture, Scorpio can become a protective parent, too. Still, they need to remember that each person has individual needs and goals. A healthy union with Scorpio involves open talks about each person's hopes, ensuring both can grow without smothering each other.

Balance is essential in Scorpio's love life. Because they can feel emotions so strongly, there is a risk of swinging between extreme closeness and distant moodiness. Partners may need to remind Scorpio that healthy love includes personal space. Sometimes, Scorpio tries to be a constant presence, worried about losing the person they love. Yet, a bit of time apart can keep things fresh and let each person remain an individual. Scorpio who learns to balance emotional depth with gentle freedom can have relationships that last a lifetime. This skill may take practice, especially if they have faced betrayal or heartbreak in the past.

Scorpio's loyalty is a bright point in love. If their partner faces a problem—health, family trouble, or even public embarrassment—Scorpio will stand by them. They might help quietly in the background, offering resources or solutions without seeking praise. This unwavering commitment can make their partner feel deeply cared for. It also means Scorpio expects the same if roles reverse. They want a partner who will not leave when times get tough. If they sense that the partner is only around for good times, Scorpio might withdraw. Real love for Scorpio includes sharing burdens as well as joys, forming a solid team of two.

Scorpio's intensity can mean that breakups are especially painful. They do not lightly toss a relationship aside. If separation happens, they might go through a deep period of mourning, reliving memories and wondering what went wrong. They can also hold onto anger if they feel betrayed. Friends or family might see them become quiet or isolated for a while. Over time, Scorpio can heal, but trust becomes harder to give in the next relationship. Some Scorpios take lessons from the breakup, growing more careful about whom they let in. Others might close off emotionally, at least until they feel someone truly respects their heart.

When happy in love, Scorpio can show a lighthearted side that others might not see. They joke around with their partner, share silly moments, or send flirty messages throughout the day. This is their way of bonding in private. Though they often have a serious reputation, they can be playful in the right situation. Partners who appreciate this mix of depth and fun often enjoy a rich emotional life with Scorpio. It is like discovering hidden treasure: beneath the calm or intense surface lies a caring heart that wants to share laughter as well as passion.

In family relationships, such as marriage with children, Scorpio might apply the same protective instincts they use in romance. They watch out for their kids, wanting them to feel safe. They might keep an eye on the child's friendships, wanting to guard them from harm. This can sometimes be seen as strict. A Scorpio parent in love with their partner may also show open displays of care, hoping to teach children that deep affection is good. However, if there is conflict, they might shield the kids from it, handling disagreements in private. Their main goal is to ensure stability, loyalty, and trust within the family home.

Scorpio may also value shared secrets with a loved one. They like having a special bond that no one else fully understands. This could be an inside joke, a hidden romantic spot, or a code phrase that sparks memories. Such secrets help Scorpio feel closer to their partner, creating a safe bubble of intimacy. This sense of "us against the world" can be a strong glue in the relationship. Still, Scorpio must be careful not to isolate their partner from friends or family. Healthy love balances private intimacy with the freedom to connect with others, maintaining trust and emotional well-being.

Each Scorpio has a unique love style, influenced by personal history and maturity. Some may cling too tightly if they have known betrayal. Others might adopt a cool exterior to test if a partner is patient. As they grow and gain self-awareness, many Scorpios learn to express love in healthier ways. They realize that letting a partner breathe does not reduce commitment. They find that gentle honesty is often more effective than sharp words. Love for Scorpio can become a transformative experience, teaching them about trust, patience, and letting go of minor worries. The right partner can help Scorpio unlock a kinder, more relaxed side of themselves.

In a long-distance relationship, Scorpio might struggle with not being physically present. They value closeness and can feel uneasy relying only on calls or texts. If they trust their partner deeply, they may manage by sharing frequent updates and planning visits. However, if doubts arise, Scorpio's imagination can run wild, leading to jealousy or fear. Clear communication is crucial. The partner should reassure Scorpio that they remain faithful. Scorpio should also stay realistic and not let hidden fears create drama. With mutual honesty and enough communication, a long-distance bond can survive. Still, Scorpio usually prefers a partner they can see more often.

Scorpio might enjoy creating romantic settings: dim lighting, soft music, and a private space. They want to engage all the senses to build a bond that feels magical. Some people call Scorpios naturally seductive, because they understand the power of ambiance and eye contact. This can excite their partner but also catch them off guard if they expected simpler dates. Scorpio invests energy in making moments special. They do not want a rushed dinner or a quick goodbye. They prefer calm, extended time together, where real feelings can emerge. This approach shows the serious side of Scorpio's desire to connect.

Gift-giving can be another way Scorpio shows affection. They might not give many small presents, but when they do, they choose carefully. The gift might link to a memory or prove they have listened to their partner's interests. At times, it can be something that hints at a private joke or a future plan. Partners often feel touched by Scorpio's thoughtful picks. Scorpio also appreciates receiving gifts that show real thought. It does not need to be expensive—maybe something homemade or an item that solves a problem they mentioned in passing. Sincere gifts, big or small, reinforce the emotional bond between them.

Friends or family might worry that Scorpio is too intense or controlling in love. If Scorpio hears such comments, they might deny it or feel misunderstood. But it can be wise to listen. Sometimes, strong feelings can slip into unhealthy control if not checked. Scorpio who learns to trust their partner and communicate openly can avoid these pitfalls. Reassuring loved ones that the relationship is built on mutual respect can help. Also, allowing the partner to keep personal friendships and hobbies is key. Scorpio's love is more stable when both sides keep their individual identity, joining together by choice rather than force.

Spiritual or emotional connections can also be part of Scorpio's love life. They might want to explore deeper meanings of life as a couple, perhaps reading about shared beliefs or attending events that spark growth. If they find a partner who shares their curious mind, the bond can strengthen. They might discuss dreams, goals, or even odd coincidences they notice. Scorpio sees love as more than just everyday events—it can be a meeting of souls. Partners who appreciate this depth can feel a rare closeness. However, if someone prefers to keep things simple and not think about bigger questions, conflicts could arise over time.

Scorpio's sense of honesty in love extends to smaller choices, like how they talk about ex-partners. They might prefer to share the basic story without hiding details if asked. But they do not want to hear continuous talk of an ex from their partner. They can become jealous or wonder if the partner still has feelings. A healthy approach is for both to address past relationships only if it helps the present. Scorpio can handle the truth, but not in a way that makes them feel second place. They want to know they are the main focus now, not overshadowed by someone from the past.

When Scorpio and a partner share goals, they can form a strong team. Whether it is saving money for a home, supporting each other's career moves, or planning travel, Scorpio invests energy in joint plans. They keep track of details, ensure deadlines are met, and look for ways to strengthen the union. Their partner might admire how Scorpio always thinks ahead. However, if the partner does not share the same direction, Scorpio can feel disappointed or left alone in their ambitions. Finding common ground helps. Sometimes, it is as simple as supporting each other's separate dreams, cheering each other on and offering helpful suggestions.

Scorpio's mood swings can affect love, especially if they feel stressed from work or personal issues. A partner might notice Scorpio becoming silent or moody without explanation. Approaching them gently can work, but if they are not ready to talk, pushing can lead to an argument. The best strategy might be, "I'm here if you want to share." Once Scorpio knows the partner respects their space, they may open up on their own. This can deepen trust, as Scorpio sees the partner is patient and kind. Over time, Scorpio might learn to voice concerns earlier, preventing heavy moods from clouding the relationship.

In social situations, a Scorpio in love can watch how their partner interacts with others. They feel proud if the partner is confident and genuine. But if the partner flirts too openly, Scorpio might feel uneasy or even jealous. Clear boundaries can prevent misunderstandings. Scorpio often wants to show the world that this is their special person, yet they also respect individuality. Partners should realize that if they cross certain lines—like giving too much attention to someone else—Scorpio might get suspicious. A calm discussion about what each sees as normal social behavior can help set the tone, ensuring both sides feel respected and secure.

For Scorpio, emotional intimacy matters as much as physical closeness. They want to feel heard when they discuss their deeper thoughts, dreams, or hidden worries. A partner who dismisses or laughs at their feelings can cause Scorpio to shut down. Scorpio opens up slowly, so they might test the partner's response to smaller admissions. If the partner responds kindly, Scorpio might share more. If the partner jokes or changes the subject, Scorpio might lock away those feelings. Over time, these missed chances can pile up. Healthy love for Scorpio includes an atmosphere where both people feel safe sharing deeper parts of who they are.

Scorpios might have strong likes and dislikes in romance. They could adore a certain type of date—like a quiet evening at home watching movies—or a special hobby they want to share. They might strongly dislike loud clubs or big social events, preferring a relaxed setting to connect. A partner who respects these preferences helps Scorpio feel comfortable. Of course, compromise is key. If the partner loves big social scenes, they might go sometimes, with Scorpio agreeing to join for shorter stays. Scorpio might, in turn, try new activities their partner enjoys. Mutual understanding and respect can keep the love dynamic and fun for both sides.

In love, Scorpio often gives direct compliments, focusing on something meaningful about the partner. They might notice how the partner's eyes light up when talking about a dream or how they always help a friend in need. These compliments mean more than typical remarks about clothing or looks. Scorpio tends to see beneath the surface and praise the soul or character. When they do this, it can deeply touch the partner. But it also sets the tone: they want that same level of depth returned. A partner who only comments on surface things might not fully grasp Scorpio's deeper, heartfelt style of connecting.

Sometimes, Scorpio may appear suspicious if a partner changes routines without explanation. For instance, if they start coming home late or texting secretly, Scorpio's mind can jump to worst-case scenarios. The partner should calmly explain what is going on to ease Scorpio's worry. Scorpio, in turn, should remember not all changes hide wrongdoing. Good communication and mutual respect for privacy help avoid drama. An anxious Scorpio might want too many details, which can feel smothering. Striking a balance between giving enough information and keeping some personal space is vital for both sides. Building this balance takes time, trust, and patience.

Scorpio can connect well with certain zodiac signs that appreciate emotional depth, loyalty, and honesty. For instance, other water signs might share the same level of feeling, though this can lead to intense ups and downs. Earth signs could provide steady grounding, helping Scorpio feel safe. Air signs might offer fresh perspectives, though Scorpio might find them too restless at times. Fire signs bring excitement but may clash if arguments flare. Of course, any match can work if both partners communicate and respect each other. Scorpio's love success depends more on shared values and honesty than just astrology. Still, these patterns might shape initial understanding.

Over time, a loving Scorpio partnership often grows deeper. The sign's persistence helps them work through arguments, provided the partner is equally committed. They might celebrate milestones privately, focusing on real meaning rather than flashy events. This approach can lead to strong emotional security. If trust remains unbroken, Scorpio might share more and more of their inner world—fears, hopes, and even childhood memories. The partner who receives these stories should handle them with care. A careless response can cause Scorpio to retreat. But a gentle, understanding reaction can cement the bond, showing Scorpio that real love allows for vulnerability without harm.

Money and finances can also affect Scorpio's love life. If they share finances with a partner, they might want clear discussions about spending, saving, or debt. They do not like surprises that undermine stability. A partner who is reckless with money might raise Scorpio's anxiety, leading to disagreements. On the other hand, if both plan together carefully, Scorpio feels safer. They might suggest joint accounts for shared bills but also keep a personal fund. This approach balances unity and independence. Talking openly about financial goals and habits can prevent hidden resentments. Scorpio values honesty in all parts of love, including money matters.

Planning for the future can bring out Scorpio's serious side. They might ask a partner about long-term goals, family plans, or where they want to live in a few years. If the partner is not ready for such talks, Scorpio can feel anxious or question the commitment level. A wise partner might explain that planning can wait until both have had more time together. Scorpio should try not to rush big steps if the relationship is still young. Yet, they appreciate at least a basic sign that the partner sees a future with them. This shared vision helps Scorpio feel secure and cherished.

A Scorpio in a stable, loving relationship can show their best qualities. They become gentle, caring, and supportive, offering a safe place for their partner to share worries or joys. They like to solve problems together and keep negativity out of the bond. In public, they might appear a bit reserved, but in private, they can be sweet or playful. If they face a challenge, they rely on the partner's honest support. This mutual reliance can form a strong couple that handles life's ups and downs as a united front. Scorpio thrives on this intense yet stable connection, feeling fulfilled when love is genuine and balanced.

Scorpio in love may sometimes need time alone to process emotions. A partner should not take this personally. It is just how Scorpio recharges. After some personal reflection, they return with a calmer mind. This is especially true after conflicts or stressful events. If the partner becomes clingy during these moments, Scorpio might feel trapped and lash out. Respecting each other's need for solitude can keep harmony. Scorpio, in return, should reassure the partner that they do not plan to vanish forever. A simple statement like, "I just need a bit of quiet time and I'll be back," can help the partner feel secure.

Family involvement can be a tricky area in Scorpio's love life. If their family meddles too much, Scorpio might push back, wanting to protect the relationship. They prefer to handle personal matters within the couple rather than letting relatives weigh in on everything. This does not mean they shut out family completely, but they draw clear lines about private issues. A partner who respects this boundary can form a good bond with Scorpio's family over time. But if family members question every choice, Scorpio might become distant or defensive. Finding a healthy balance between family ties and the couple's own decisions is key.

Some Scorpios have a talent for sensing emotional undercurrents. They notice if their partner is sad or annoyed, even if the partner tries to hide it. They might say, "What's on your mind?" or "Are you okay?" This can be comforting, as the partner feels understood. However, it can also feel like pressure if the partner wants to keep some emotions private for a while. Scorpios should respect that not everyone is ready to talk immediately. A partner who says, "I just need a bit of time," is not necessarily withholding trust; they might simply handle stress differently. Over time, love grows when both methods are accepted.

Romantic getaways or short trips can bring out Scorpio's desire for privacy and depth. They might plan a secluded cabin stay or a quiet beach trip rather than a crowded city tour. They want one-on-one time to bond, talk, and explore. This is where they can truly relax and let walls down. Partners who enjoy these shared escapes might find Scorpio opening up in new ways. The peaceful setting can encourage open talks or simply a restful togetherness. If the partner prefers very busy vacations, they might compromise by splitting time between exploring and relaxing, ensuring both get what they need out of the trip.

Handling heartbreak is a big test for Scorpio. They feel love so deeply that a breakup can shake their sense of security. Some Scorpios retreat from romance for a long while, focusing on personal healing or throwing themselves into work or hobbies. Others might keep re-checking old memories, struggling to let go. Supportive friends or therapy can help them process pain. They must remember that one failed bond does not define their worth. With time, many Scorpios emerge stronger, more careful in choosing partners but still open to the power of love. They learn that trust is a gift, not a guarantee, and they become wiser from the experience.

As years pass in a stable relationship, Scorpio might deepen their commitment in ways that do not always show outwardly. They might handle more shared finances, quietly help their partner with big decisions, or manage important documents. The partner might look back and realize how much Scorpio has done behind the scenes. This quiet support can be comforting. However, Scorpio should be sure they do not take on everything alone. Love flourishes when both partners share duties and responsibilities. When they communicate well about who does what, they avoid resentment or burnout. This solid partnership can keep the spark alive through mutual respect and teamwork.

Cultural or family traditions in love can matter to Scorpio if they see genuine meaning in them. They might be drawn to symbolic rituals that represent fidelity or emotional depth. However, they dislike any tradition that feels hollow or forced. They may adapt customs to fit their real beliefs. If the partner's culture is different, Scorpio can be curious, wanting to learn the significance. They might embrace certain parts wholeheartedly if they resonate with loyalty and devotion. This can bring the couple closer, weaving shared values into their love story. Scorpio's approach: keep what is sincere, avoid what is just for show.

Scorpio loves to celebrate relationship milestones in private, heartfelt ways. They might mark an anniversary or special date with a handwritten note, a homemade meal, or a thoughtful trip. Rather than a huge party, they prefer time alone with the partner. They might reflect on how far they have come together or recall favorite moments. This does not mean they never attend big events, but the real meaning for Scorpio often lies in the smaller, more intimate gestures. These quiet celebrations can strengthen emotional ties, reminding both people of why they stand together. It is a personal approach that shows Scorpio's deep, caring nature.

Jealousy can rear its head if Scorpio feels the partner is drifting away, or if they see suspicious behavior. The best approach is open and calm communication. The partner should explain their perspective, reassure Scorpio of their commitment, and not dismiss Scorpio's feelings as silly. Scorpio, in turn, must recognize that trust means giving the partner freedom, not monitoring every move. Couples who handle jealousy maturely can grow stronger. They learn that real loyalty comes from mutual respect and honesty, not from heavy-handed control. Over time, Scorpio can relax, seeing that a loved one's independence does not threaten the bond.

Overall, Scorpio's love style is one of devotion, honesty, and intensity. They dive deeply into relationships, seeking profound emotional ties rather than surface-level bonds. Their loyalty can be unwavering, but they do expect the same in return. While this can create dramatic moments, it can also form relationships that withstand hardships. Scorpio's partner should be ready for open talks, strong passion, and the occasional need for privacy. If both sides practice trust, patience, and honesty, the love that develops can be incredibly fulfilling. Scorpio's heart, once opened, brings warmth, protection, and dedication to a union that can stand the test of time.

CHAPTER 11: SCORPIO AND COMMUNICATION

Scorpios have a thoughtful style when it comes to communication. They might not speak first or reveal their opinions right away. Instead, they observe what others say and do, then decide how to respond. This careful approach can make them seem reserved in group chats or at the start of a conversation. However, when they feel comfortable, they can share insights that show how much they have been paying attention. Their communication style often revolves around being accurate and clear. They do not like to waste words. If they have something to say, they want it to carry meaning.

While some individuals speak loudly to grab attention, Scorpios typically prefer a quieter tone. This does not mean they are shy. Instead, they might speak with a calm voice that draws people in. When they do raise their volume, it usually signals something important. They tend to avoid empty chatter, so their words can have a real impact. Their sense of privacy also affects how they share information. They protect personal details and expect others to respect that boundary. If a Scorpio senses that someone is prying, they might keep answers short and steer the subject away from sensitive areas.

In one-on-one conversations, Scorpios often make strong eye contact. This can feel intense to some people, but it is part of Scorpio's way of focusing on the person they are talking with. They want to catch small cues in tone or facial expressions. This helps them gauge if the other person is being genuine. On the flip side, if they sense someone is lying, they may become distant or ask pointed questions. For Scorpios, communication is not just about words; it is about the truth behind them. Their watchful eyes and careful listening allow them to detect any mismatch between word and emotion.

Because Scorpios do not always share everything at once, misunderstandings can arise. Someone might think Scorpio is angry or upset, when in fact they are just deep in thought. If this happens often, it can create tension. Scorpios can help by offering small clarifications or a friendly comment, letting others know they are not irritated. Others, in turn, can learn to read Scorpio's signals better. A simple, "I am just thinking things over," can clear up confusion. Open communication can reduce the guesswork. Still, Scorpios like to keep some thoughts private, so they usually balance honesty with a measure of reserve.

When Scorpios do speak openly, their words can be powerful. They might surprise friends or coworkers with a direct statement, a clever observation, or a detailed plan. Because they keep ideas in their mind before talking, they often present them with thorough reasoning. This can earn them respect in workplace meetings or family discussions. However, it can also catch others off guard if they expected the Scorpio to remain silent. Scorpios do not necessarily talk more as they get comfortable, but the quality of what they say might reveal how much they truly know or have thought about a topic.

Scorpios prefer honest and meaningful exchanges. They are not fans of shallow flattery or exaggerations. If they sense someone is being false, they might respond by asking sharp questions. This can be intimidating for those who are not used to Scorpio's style. Yet, for people who value truthful conversation, it can be refreshing. Scorpios might also show interest in serious subjects such as psychology, mysteries, history, or anything that involves going beneath the surface. They like to discover real motivations behind actions. Because of this, they ask questions that can feel intense or personal, though they usually respect boundaries if asked.

In group settings, Scorpio might remain an observer at first. They notice who talks the most, who interrupts, and who seems to hold back. If the group is lively, Scorpio might speak less until they feel the moment is right. Some might label them as quiet, but Scorpio is simply assessing the situation. When they do jump in, they often shift the direction of the chat with a thoughtful point or a direct question. This can either guide the group to deeper ideas or, at times, make those seeking light banter a bit uncomfortable. Still, Scorpio's approach can be valuable for real problem-solving.

Scorpios usually dislike gossip. They find it unproductive and dishonest, especially if it involves half-truths. If they hear rumors or see coworkers whispering, they may keep out of it. Sometimes, they might call out the behavior if it damages someone's reputation unfairly. Their own preference is to speak directly to a person about any concerns. This can reduce misunderstandings, though it does require courage. If a Scorpio friend hears something negative about another friend, they might check facts before believing it. Their respect for truth extends to defending others from unfair stories. This can build trust among those who appreciate sincerity.

Listening skills are another aspect of Scorpio's communication style. Though they might not appear warm and fuzzy, they often pay close attention to what is being said. They pick up on subtle changes in voice or emphasis. If a friend shares a personal problem, Scorpio may not react with big emotional gestures, but they file away important details. Later, they might offer practical help or advice that proves they listened carefully. This can be a surprise for people who thought Scorpio was aloof. In reality, Scorpios just prefer to show they care through follow-up actions, not always through immediate, visible sympathy.

Conflict resolution can be challenging for Scorpio. If they feel wronged, they may withdraw and think about it for a while instead of addressing it immediately. They might wait until they have all the facts before responding. When they do respond, it can be direct. Some conflicts can be solved quickly if the other person is also honest. But if the other person evades the issue or denies wrongdoing, Scorpio might persist with pointed questions. This can escalate tension. A calmer approach could involve Scorpio sharing how they feel, then offering a chance for the other person to speak. Finding common ground can prevent grudges.

Written communication also reflects Scorpio's style. They may write concise emails or messages, focusing on the main points. They generally dislike writing long, flowery notes unless the content deserves it. This directness can be helpful in professional settings. However, in personal chats, some may misread Scorpio's brevity as a lack of interest. In reality, they just prefer to get straight to the point. If they are comfortable with someone, they might add a personal touch or thoughtful remark. But overall, their writing mirrors their spoken habits: measured, clear, and not overly chatty unless they see a real reason to expand.

Scorpios are skilled at reading body language. A tilt of the head, a slight frown, or a shift in posture can tell them if a person feels uneasy. They use these clues to adjust how they speak. If they see fear, they might soften their tone. If they see someone is hiding something, they might ask a follow-up question. This can make them strong negotiators or mediators. Still, they must watch that they do not become too probing. Not everyone likes being observed so closely. But for Scorpio, these observations are a natural part of connecting. They see each conversation as a puzzle to understand.

Trust is vital for Scorpio's communication. They open up more when they feel certain the other person will not use their words against them. If a friend or partner shares Scorpio's private thoughts without permission, Scorpio might shut down. They can become guarded or even decide never to reveal personal matters again. In a close relationship where trust is strong, Scorpio can be expressive, sharing feelings and hopes that few others hear. In this environment, their communication style shifts from reserved to engaged. They enjoy deep talks about life, the future, or personal beliefs, but only when the foundation of trust is secure.

In educational or training settings, Scorpios might ask many questions if the topic interests them. They want to dig beneath the surface rather than accept simple answers. This can make them good students or trainees, although instructors might find their questions challenging. If the topic feels shallow or not explained well, Scorpio can seem uninterested. They do not see the point in repeating facts without understanding the reasons behind them. Classmates or fellow trainees might appreciate Scorpio's probing, because it can lead to a better grasp of the subject. However, they might also feel uncomfortable if they prefer to stay on superficial ideas.

Humor for Scorpio can be dry or subtle. They might crack a joke in a deadpan style, leaving others unsure if they are serious. Those who know Scorpio's sense of humor may find this hilarious, while newcomers might feel puzzled. In close friendships, Scorpios might poke fun in a gentle way, testing whether the other person picks up on their wit. They appreciate clever humor that has a bit of insight. However, they might not enjoy jokes that rely on bullying or spreading untrue stories. Their strong sense of fairness extends to laughter as well, so they avoid mocking people in mean ways.

When dealing with emotions, Scorpios might use communication to protect themselves. They share their worries only after they have tested the waters. If they sense a person will handle their confessions with care, they speak more freely. If not, they stay silent. This can cause friction if loved ones expect immediate openness. Patience works best. Over time, Scorpio can learn that expressing concerns earlier might prevent misunderstandings. Still, their natural inclination is to wait until they feel certain. This method, while cautious, can be misunderstood by those who see it as a lack of trust. Clarifying the reasons for this caution can help.

Online communication with a Scorpio might mirror their face-to-face style. They do not usually post every detail of their life, preferring to keep personal matters off social media. They might only share important updates or small glimpses. In direct messages, they keep it cordial but concise. They might open up if it is someone they trust, perhaps sending a longer message about a deep topic. However, they usually avoid public arguments or attention-seeking posts. If someone tries to stir drama online, Scorpio might block or ignore them. They do not see the point in airing personal disputes in a public space.

Some people might find Scorpio's communication style too intense. Others appreciate how real it can be. Scorpios strive to cut through nonsense and reach the core of an issue. This approach helps them solve problems quickly, but it can also unsettle people who prefer softer methods. Scorpios can adapt by reading the room. If they sense their directness is creating anxiety, they can slow down and use more gentle phrasing. At the same time, others can learn that Scorpio's strong presence is not meant to scare anyone. It is simply how they engage with the world: focusing on truth and pushing aside superficial layers.

When guiding younger people, such as children or teens, Scorpios might speak simply yet firmly. They do not make false promises and expect the same honesty in return. A Scorpio parent or mentor might ask questions to help the younger person understand their own thoughts. For example, "Why do you think that?" or "How can we solve this problem together?" This encourages the child or teen to think deeply rather than just accept instructions. The young person might feel challenged but also respected. As a result, they might open up to Scorpio more than they would to someone who dismisses their opinions.

Overall, Scorpio's communication style is shaped by depth, observation, and sincerity. They do not talk simply to fill silence. They prefer honest exchanges and guard their own personal details until they feel safe. This might make them appear reserved, but it also helps them speak with real clarity when needed. Their ability to read body language and tone allows them to respond in a way that cuts to the heart of the issue. While they can come across as intense, they are simply seeking truth. With respect, patience, and trust on both sides, Scorpio can form meaningful connections that last.

CHAPTER 12: SCORPIO AND DAILY ROUTINES

Scorpios often thrive when they develop routines that fit their focused personalities. While some people enjoy changing schedules, Scorpios typically like knowing when certain tasks will happen. Having structure can help them channel their energy toward important goals. Their day might start with quiet moments, such as reading or checking messages privately before facing the world. During these early moments, they can plan how they will approach responsibilities. This steady start helps them avoid feeling rushed. Some Scorpios may prefer a later wake-up if they are night owls. Either way, they often settle into a pattern that suits their natural rhythm.

Because of Scorpio's water element, they might feel energized or calm when they incorporate water into daily routines. For instance, a Scorpio might savor a morning shower or bath, seeing it as a time to clear their mind before the day's demands. Others might end the night with a soak or a warm rinse to wash away tensions. They might also enjoy sipping tea or staying hydrated throughout the day. This focus on water can be subtle, but it can help them maintain balance. While not every Scorpio has these habits, many feel a link to water that soothes their often intense emotions.

Scorpios can be determined in managing responsibilities. If they have a deadline at school or work, they might organize tasks into smaller steps, tackling each one carefully. This sense of order can extend to chores or home duties. For example, they might pick a specific day to do laundry or a certain evening to tidy up personal spaces. Having a consistent time for these tasks helps them feel in control. When they do skip a planned task, they can become uneasy, as if something is off. While they might adjust spontaneously if needed, they prefer to stick to what they have set out to do.

Physical health can hold a key place in Scorpio's routine. Because they handle stress deeply, they often feel better if they release tension through exercise or mindful movement. Some Scorpios enjoy solitary workouts, like running alone or practicing gentle stretching in a quiet corner. Others might join structured classes, appreciating the set schedule. Either way, they tend to keep their fitness plans to themselves. They may not post daily gym selfies, but they keep track of progress. This approach matches their habit of doing things seriously yet privately. They might experiment until they find the best way to stay physically strong and emotionally grounded.

In terms of meals, some Scorpios pick a consistent eating schedule. They might eat at the same times daily, focusing on balanced portions. Others prefer a more flexible approach, but still aim for quality. They might enjoy cooking at home, where they can control ingredients. If they live with family or roommates, they might have a set day when they prepare dinner for everyone. When dining out, they often seek places with deeper flavors rather than just quick snacks. This is not about being fancy; it is about savoring tastes that match their intense nature. They also appreciate mealtimes as a pause in a busy schedule.

For Scorpios who work or study, daily routines often revolve around productivity. They may block out specific hours to focus on projects, turning off distractions. Once they commit to a task, they dive in until they reach a stopping point. If others break their concentration with random demands, Scorpio can become irritated. Setting boundaries is important, so they might let family or coworkers know when they should not be disturbed. This level of discipline can help

Scorpios excel in complex tasks. They keep track of details, follow up on pending actions, and revisit goals to make sure nothing is overlooked.

Break times can be a hidden part of Scorpio's day that is crucial for their mental health. Though they are determined, they cannot work nonstop without rest. Some might schedule short breaks, using the time to stretch, step outside for fresh air, or simply close their eyes and breathe. If a Scorpio does not take these breaks, their mind can become overwhelmed, leading to irritability or tension. They might also guard these breaks so no one can intrude. During that period, they may check a personal list, read a few pages of a book, or do something else that feels quietly refreshing.

Sleep is another key factor. Scorpios might struggle if they do not get enough rest. Their active minds can run late into the night, especially if they have unresolved thoughts. As a result, they might adopt a bedtime ritual to wind down. This can involve dimming lights, listening to soft music, or writing in a journal. If they share a space, they might need quiet after a certain hour. Some Scorpios like to keep a window slightly open for fresh air, tying back to their water sign trait of enjoying a calm environment. They usually treasure uninterrupted sleep, as it helps them recharge deeply.

On weekends or free days, Scorpios may keep a different routine. They might skip the early alarm and spend time on personal projects or hobbies. Others might plan private outings or catch up with a small group of trusted friends. Because they value privacy, they might not fill their free time with large social events. Instead, they focus on doing things that bring them a sense of renewal. This can include reading books about intriguing topics, researching a subject that caught their interest, or exploring a local spot that feels peaceful. They see downtime as a chance to reconnect with their inner self.

Many Scorpios have a curious mind, so part of their daily routine might involve learning. This could be reading an article, listening to a podcast, or following a short online course. They like to expand their knowledge, especially in areas that allow them to uncover hidden layers—be it science, history, or practical skills like repairing items. They might dedicate a set time each day to this pursuit. Even if it is just 15 minutes, they appreciate the sense of growth it brings. Over time, these small learning sessions accumulate, helping them become well-informed and confident in their chosen areas of interest.

Scorpios may keep a personal planner, journal, or digital calendar. This helps them remember important events, track their goals, or note down ideas that occur during the day. They usually do not show this planner to others, seeing it as private. But inside, it might have color codes or special markings that reflect their priorities. They might write short reflections, such as what they accomplished or something that frustrated them. By doing so, they can spot patterns in their mood or routine. Over time, this awareness can lead them to adjust daily habits for better results or to avoid burnout.

Some Scorpios also enjoy having a small corner at home where they organize tasks. This could be a desk in a quiet room or even a specific chair. Surrounding themselves with items that spark focus—like a lamp, a favorite pen, or certain objects—can make that area feel like a personal zone of productivity. They usually keep it tidy because clutter can distract them. If family members or roommates wander in, Scorpio might politely ask for space. They see this corner as a safe bubble to concentrate on tasks or reflect without interruption. Having such a spot can be a big factor in their daily flow.

Motivation can sometimes fluctuate for Scorpio, as they experience strong emotions. If they wake up feeling upset or drained, it can affect their routine. They might push themselves to keep going, but they also know that acknowledging moods is vital. Some days, they might shorten tasks or adjust the schedule to allow more rest. Others might include a comforting activity, such as a short walk, to reset their mind. This flexibility can prevent negative feelings from building up. While they like structure, they also realize that forcing themselves to follow a rigid schedule can lead to emotional strain. Balancing discipline with self-care is key.

Routines around technology can also shape a Scorpio's day. They might set specific times to check emails or scroll through social media. They know how easy it is to fall into constant phone use, which can distract from deeper tasks. Some limit notifications or use apps that block distractions while they work or study. This approach helps them preserve mental clarity. If they do engage in online platforms, they prefer meaningful interactions or valuable information. They might also store important data in well-labeled folders on their devices, reflecting their inclination for order. Being mindful about digital habits ensures they stay productive and calm.

Relaxation in the evening might involve music or a calming hobby. A Scorpio could spend an hour listening to tunes that match their mood, or they might choose something instrumental to soothe their thoughts. They might also enjoy journaling about the day, writing any lingering ideas or feelings. Others might prefer a puzzle, a strategy game, or a short session of reading mysterious novels. This period is meant to gently transition them from work to rest. By focusing on a personal interest, they allow their intense mind to settle down. Loved ones can support this by respecting their need for quiet time.

For Scorpios who have children, daily routines can become more complex. They might build the family schedule around the children's needs while still carving out some space for themselves. For instance, they could wake up earlier to have personal quiet time before helping the kids get ready for school. Throughout the day, they keep track of homework, mealtimes, and bedtime stories. Even with these responsibilities, they try to maintain a sense of order. They might plan a weekly meal chart or an activity list. This helps Scorpio manage the household without feeling overwhelmed. It also reassures the children that life has reliable patterns.

Sometimes, unexpected events disrupt Scorpio's well-laid plans. A sudden assignment at work, a friend needing help, or a personal emergency can throw them off balance. Initially, they might feel stressed because they did not anticipate the change. However, once they get a grip on the new situation, they can adapt. Their resourceful nature kicks in, allowing them to rearrange tasks or find clever solutions. After the dust settles, they often reflect on how they handled it and update their routines if needed. This shows that while they enjoy stability, they are not rigid. They can bend to life's surprises while keeping their core habits intact.

Boundaries play a big role in Scorpio's day. They do not like people barging into their personal time or space. To maintain boundaries, they might lock their office door when working on sensitive tasks or turn off their phone when they need to focus. This can seem standoffish, but it is simply how they protect their mental energy. Once they finish, they may return calls or messages, being more open. Family or roommates who understand Scorpio's need for boundaries usually have fewer conflicts about it. By respecting these limits, everyone benefits, and Scorpio can carry out tasks without feeling constantly interrupted.

Certain Scorpios might include spiritual or reflective activities in their day. This could be a short prayer, a meditation, or a moment of quiet contemplation. They might not speak about it openly, seeing it as personal. But this practice helps them stay grounded, especially since their emotions can run deep. If they skip these moments, they might feel unsettled. In some cases, they might do something like keep a gratitude list or read a short meaningful passage. These small rituals can center them, reminding them to manage stress and connect with what truly matters. Over time, this can enhance their sense of inner peace.

Overall, Scorpio's daily routines reflect their desire for steady organization, personal privacy, and mindful living. They often map out tasks, set times for exercise or chores, and embrace small moments of rest to keep their energy balanced. While they thrive on structure, they also make room for reflection and emotional well-being. If life throws a curveball, they adjust carefully, determined to maintain order. This blend of discipline and adaptability supports Scorpio's strong focus, helping them reach goals without sacrificing inner calm. By honoring their own rhythms and setting healthy boundaries, Scorpios craft a daily life that aligns with their thoughtful, powerful nature.

CHAPTER 13: SCORPIO WITH GROUPS

Scorpios can be interesting members of any group because of their watchful nature and desire for truth. When they join a club, team, or larger gathering, they usually observe first rather than rush into the spotlight. Some people see this as being shy, but it is more about figuring out who everyone is and how they act. Scorpios prefer to avoid mistakes that come from moving too fast. Once they feel more confident, they contribute to the group in thoughtful ways. They will support ideas they believe in and question those that seem questionable. Their presence can bring depth to group activities.

In study groups or academic clubs, Scorpios tend to focus on the facts and thorough understanding of the topic. They might be the one who digs for extra research material or asks the tough questions that no one else has considered. Some group members appreciate this, as it helps everyone learn more. Others might find it intense or feel challenged by Scorpio's probing mind. However, Scorpios do not ask questions to show off. They do it because they want the group to be accurate. If the group is open to deeper analysis, Scorpio can become a valuable contributor to projects and discussions.

In social clubs, such as community groups or hobby circles, Scorpios usually gravitate toward the members who share their specific interests. They do not aim to be everyone's friend. Instead, they prefer a few closer bonds within the group. If it is a photography club, they might spend time discussing camera settings or editing tips with someone equally serious about improving. If it is a gardening society, they could learn new techniques for growing special plants. Their willingness to exchange knowledge makes them respected by those who see the same value in digging deeper. Over time, these smaller bonds can strengthen group connections.

When a Scorpio enters a new group, they often take mental notes about the personalities involved. They look for potential friends and also watch for those who spread gossip or break trust. This approach can keep them from sharing personal information too early. Many Scorpios prefer to keep details about their private life quiet until they know who is truly loyal. In a large group, they might hang back, speak politely, and learn the group's unwritten rules. Once they feel comfortable, they might contribute more frequently, possibly suggesting new ideas or taking on tasks that match their skills. They become more active once trust is built.

In team sports or group performances, Scorpios can display determination. They want to succeed, both personally and for the group. If it is a sports team, a Scorpio might train consistently, encouraging teammates to do the same. If it is a dance group or a theater troupe, they will practice diligently. But they do not show off; they simply want to master their part. Some teammates appreciate Scorpio's commitment, while others might feel it adds pressure. Scorpio's focus on the end goal can help the group win or perform well. However, they can be strict if they see someone not giving their best effort.

Because Scorpios value honesty, they can clash with people who act unfairly or bend rules in group settings. For example, if someone tries to take credit for another's work, Scorpio might call it out. This directness can feel uncomfortable to those who prefer to avoid confrontation. Yet, it can preserve fairness and mutual respect within the group. Many come to see Scorpio as a protector of fair play, especially if the group has a tendency to let small dishonesties slide. Scorpio's stance might not always be popular, but it can help maintain a healthier dynamic where members trust each other more.

Scorpios often adapt their communication style depending on the group's purpose. In a professional group, such as a business meeting or a volunteer committee, they present their points clearly, focusing on the facts. In a casual group, like a game night with friends, they might relax and show their quieter humor. Still, they keep an eye on how the group behaves. If the group setting becomes too chaotic or superficial, Scorpio may lose interest and either leave or withdraw. On the other hand, if the environment supports open discussion, they can become more involved, offering insights that push the group to think more deeply.

Scorpios sometimes take on leadership roles in groups, but not always by choice. Their steady manner, combined with an ability to see hidden issues, can make others look to them for guidance. If they accept a leadership position, they run a tight ship. They might assign tasks based on who is best at each job and set strict deadlines. This works well for organized groups that appreciate structure. However, groups that prefer a laid-back style might find Scorpio's approach too controlling. If the group and Scorpio align on the importance of goals, it can be a productive match. Scorpio leads calmly, trusting those who prove reliable.

When conflicts arise in a group, Scorpio tends to remain calm on the surface, even if they feel strong emotions inside. They watch how people argue, noting who exaggerates or changes facts. After collecting enough observations, Scorpio might step in with direct questions or clarifications. Their goal is to uncover the root of the disagreement. Some group members might feel uneasy under Scorpio's intense stare, but it can help bring real issues into the open. If Scorpio believes a solution is possible, they will guide the group toward a fair compromise. If not, they may quietly support the side they see as just.

Group decision-making can be tricky for Scorpio. They usually do not speak up just to blend in with popular opinion. Instead, they voice what they truly think, which can go against the majority if they see flaws in the plan. If the group ignores Scorpio's warnings and things go wrong later, Scorpio might not say "I told you so," but they will remember how events unfolded. In future decisions, they might be even more cautious about trusting group consensus. Still, if the group is open-minded and listens to Scorpio's concerns, they can avoid common mistakes and produce stronger outcomes together.

Social gatherings, like parties or events with many people, can be challenging for a private Scorpio. They might find a corner or a small circle to talk with, rather than floating around. Observing the bigger scene helps them decide if they want to engage or not. If conversations revolve around trivial topics for too long, Scorpio may feel bored. Yet, if they find someone who enjoys deeper talk, they might settle in and have a meaningful one-on-one. By the end of the event, they might have formed one or two genuine connections instead of collecting a lot of superficial contacts.

In activist groups or volunteer efforts, Scorpios can be very dedicated if they strongly believe in the cause. They do not seek attention for doing good. Instead, they prefer behind-the-scenes roles where they can plan strategies or do research. They might handle tasks that require focus, like organizing data or contacting people privately. If the group has a shared mission that speaks to Scorpio's sense of right and wrong, they can commit long hours. However, if they see group leaders acting dishonestly, they might confront them or leave the group entirely. They cannot support a cause that uses unethical methods.

Scorpios in family groups, like extended family gatherings, may stick to a few relatives they trust. They tend to avoid gossiping relatives who pry into personal matters. If a big family dinner happens, Scorpio might help in practical ways, such as setting the table or organizing tasks. But they might not jump into every conversation. Relatives who know them well might try to involve them gently. Scorpio appreciates respectful invitations but will still pick which chats to join. They protect their privacy even in family circles, sharing personal updates only with those who have proven to keep things confidential.

For Scorpio children in school groups, they might be the ones who quietly keep the group on track. Even if they do not speak a lot, they notice which classmates do their part and which slack off. If they sense unfairness—like someone copying work—they can get frustrated. Teachers might see them as serious or introverted, but they can encourage the child to share ideas. The Scorpio child might open up if they trust the teacher's fairness. In group projects, they do their tasks well and hope others do the same. If the group fails, the Scorpio child may feel disappointed but learn who they can rely on next time.

Online groups can be a different world. Scorpios might join forums or social media groups for specific interests, such as cooking, reading, or learning new skills. They prefer to observe the tone of these groups before posting. If members are respectful and share real knowledge, Scorpio might engage with detailed comments or advice. If the group is full of mean or dishonest behavior, they might leave quietly. Online arguments do not appeal to them. When they do participate, they offer well-thought-out contributions. This can lead to in-depth discussions that others find helpful. Over time, they build a reputation for reliability and sincerity in these communities.

In professional networking groups, Scorpios use their careful approach to spot genuine connections rather than just collecting business cards. They might attend gatherings that focus on smaller, focused conversations rather than huge meet-and-greet events. At a networking lunch, for example, they might chat with a few people who show true interest in their field, exchanging deeper insights. This can result in strong professional bonds. However, if the environment feels full of shallow talk or bragging, Scorpio may make a polite excuse to leave. They see no point in forced networking. The connections they do form often turn into lasting professional relationships built on shared values.

Scorpio's resourcefulness becomes clear in group planning. Whether it is organizing a fundraiser or a group trip, they anticipate possible issues in advance. They might research permits, check weather patterns, or verify schedules to ensure everything runs smoothly. If something goes wrong, Scorpio quickly looks for solutions. That might mean calling a backup venue or contacting someone who can fix a technical glitch. Group members who recognize Scorpio's foresight appreciate having them around. Over time, many groups learn to involve Scorpio in the early stages of planning. This saves time and reduces crises, making Scorpio an unofficial problem-solver that everyone respects.

In creative groups, like art clubs or writing circles, Scorpios might propose unusual themes or deeper projects. They enjoy exploring subjects that reveal hidden truths or emotional layers. Some members may love Scorpio's bold ideas, while others might prefer safer paths. If the group is open-minded, Scorpio's suggestions can lead to powerful works that stand out. However, if the group is cautious and does not want to push boundaries, Scorpio could feel limited. They might continue working independently while participating only as much as needed. Ideally, they find a creative group that appreciates passion, letting Scorpio's energy drive innovative projects forward.

Group celebrations can be a mixed bag for Scorpio. If the group decides to mark an achievement, Scorpio might join in but keep a low profile. They do not usually enjoy large fusses, even if they contributed a lot to the success. They prefer smaller acknowledgments with close teammates or a private sense of satisfaction. If the group demands everyone stand on stage or share personal stories, Scorpio might feel awkward. They do not want to overshadow others or reveal too much about themselves. Therefore, they might quietly slip away once the formalities end, leaving others to continue the festivities if they wish.

Overall, Scorpio's approach to group dynamics combines caution, depth, and integrity. They take time to decide how much to reveal about themselves, and they want to see if the group shares their values of honesty and respect. Once they trust the group, they become steady contributors who offer practical help and thoughtful insights. They do not crave constant attention, but they do care about real teamwork. If someone acts unfairly or tries to manipulate the group, Scorpio will notice and may confront the issue head-on. Their presence can keep a group balanced, pushing it to aim higher and maintain genuine bonds.

CHAPTER 14: NOTABLE PEOPLE WITH SCORPIO BIRTHDAYS

People born between October 23 and November 21 are often labeled Scorpios, and many well-known figures share these birth dates. Whether they are authors, scientists, performers, leaders, or athletes, they tend to display qualities linked with Scorpio traits: determination, depth, and a focus on reaching big goals. While we must remember that sun signs alone do not dictate personality, it can be interesting to see how some Scorpio characteristics show up in the lives of famous individuals. Their stories can inspire fans who notice the same type of determination or quiet intensity in themselves. Let us explore a few of these notable Scorpios.

One example is the famous painter Pablo Picasso, born on October 25. His work broke many artistic boundaries. Though he is sometimes linked with a different sign by older calendars, many still view him as a late-October Scorpio. Picasso demonstrated a daring approach to art, shifting styles throughout his life and defying norms. This kind of boldness can echo a Scorpio's readiness to transform or reinvent themselves. He also showed fierce focus: producing thousands of works over decades. Some might see his approach as intense, a word often connected to Scorpio. Indeed, Picasso's passion for creativity and his private nature align well with Scorpio themes.

Scientist Marie Curie, born on November 7, is another notable figure who sometimes appears on Scorpio lists, though historical note may place her birth under older date systems. She exemplified strong will and a pursuit of deeper knowledge—traits often linked with Scorpio. Curie researched radioactivity and won two Nobel Prizes, showing her relentless drive in an era when women faced many barriers in science. Her dedication to discovery, even working in unsafe conditions by modern standards, suggests the fearless side sometimes ascribed to Scorpio. She quietly yet powerfully changed how we see the atomic world, a testament to the sign's reputation for uncovering hidden truths.

Another celebrated figure with a Scorpio birthday is Bill Gates (October 28). Known for co-founding Microsoft, Gates played a huge part in shaping personal computers and software. Scorpio's focus on strategy and problem-solving is easy to spot in his approach to business. Despite fierce competition, he steadily guided Microsoft to worldwide success. Even after stepping away from leading the company, he continued to apply a determined mindset to philanthropic efforts. Through his foundation, he addresses global health issues, which aligns with Scorpio's ability to tackle deep-rooted problems. Gates's calm demeanor, combined with careful planning, mirrors the Scorpio combination of quiet observation and decisive action.

Musician and singer-songwriter Katy Perry, born October 25, has also displayed Scorpio-like qualities in her career. Known for bold performance styles and strong themes in her music, she has not shied away from expressing intense emotions or personal challenges. Her transformation from a gospel singer to a pop star might reflect Scorpio's capacity for reinvention. In interviews, she often speaks about serious topics, such as self-worth and growth, hinting at a deeper layer beneath her public pop image. While people's personalities are shaped by many factors, fans can see glimpses of Scorpio's passion, determination, and willingness to explore personal truths in her work.

Actor Leonardo DiCaprio, born November 11, is often cited as a Scorpio. He is recognized for taking on roles that require emotional depth and intensity, from troubled characters to historic figures. DiCaprio's career path shows a desire for quality over quantity, carefully selecting projects that push him to new heights. This search for depth can line up with Scorpio's preference for meaningful experiences. Off-screen, he supports environmental causes, another sign of the heartfelt commitment that Scorpios can exhibit when they believe in something strongly. His private personal life also fits the Scorpio pattern of drawing a line between public work and private matters.

Another Scorpio name that often appears is Ryan Gosling, born November 12. Known for both dramatic and lighter roles, Gosling tends to keep a certain distance from the media, which matches the Scorpio trait of valuing privacy. He speaks carefully about personal or family matters, sharing only what he chooses. His acting choices, from romance to thrilling drama, show a willingness to dive into challenging scripts that reveal different sides of human emotion. Fans often sense a quiet intensity in his performances, a hallmark that can be traced back to Scorpio's deep well of feeling. His measured, calm public persona underlines this as well.

In the realm of sports, there are also well-known Scorpio figures. For instance, Brazilian soccer star Pelé was born on October 23. He is widely regarded as one of the greatest soccer players in history. Pelé's remarkable goal-scoring ability, combined with his devotion to improving his skills, showed the kind of unstoppable drive associated with Scorpio. Off the field, he often advocated for sports as a way to bring positive change, reflecting a deeper concern for social issues. Scorpios can show fierce determination in competition, and Pelé's achievements, including multiple World Cup wins, highlight that strong sense of purpose.

Another sports personality sometimes listed under Scorpio is figure skater Tonya Harding, born November 12. Known for her powerful skating and the controversies around her career, Harding displayed a relentless push toward success in a highly competitive field. She executed moves like the triple axel, a jump few female skaters attempted at the time. The swirling media attention around her personal life and the infamous incident with Nancy Kerrigan highlight how intense a Scorpio storyline can become, though it is important to remember the complexities of real events. Harding's fierce ambition and complicated narrative can reflect the extremes Scorpio may face when under pressure.

In political spheres, many leaders have birthdays that place them under Scorpio, each with different degrees of intensity. One example is Hilary Rodham Clinton, born October 26. Known for her long career in law and public service, she exemplifies a strong will to continue pursuing goals despite setbacks. Whether people agree or disagree with her politics, they can see her resilience in the face of challenges—an aspect often noted in Scorpios. She also keeps much of her personal life guarded, showing a Scorpio-like preference for privacy. The seriousness of her public work, along with her perseverance, lines up with common Scorpio traits.

Musician and performer Drake, born on October 24, also appears on Scorpio lists. Originally known for an acting role on a teen drama, he later shifted fully to music and soared to international fame. His lyrics often delve into personal emotions, relationships, and introspection, which fans interpret as signs of Scorpio's depth. Drake's continuous effort to evolve musically, from rap to pop elements, might show that Scorpio style of transformation. While he enjoys sharing parts of his life publicly, he remains strategic about certain details, giving glimpses of the protective boundary a Scorpio sets between the outer image and inner self.

Another example is actress and humanitarian Anne Hathaway, born November 12. She is recognized for choosing varied roles—some light, some deeply challenging—and for her dedication to causes such as gender equality. Her shift from early family-friendly films to more serious parts could reflect that Scorpio sense of growth. In interviews, Hathaway has shown a thoughtful approach to her work, discussing how she immerses herself in roles. This immersion can link to Scorpio's characteristic intensity. Off-screen, she keeps many aspects of her family life private, suggesting a guarded side. Fans often see her as both warm and quietly determined, aligning with a gentler expression of Scorpio energy.

Musical legend Neil Young, born November 12, has often been praised for his passion and sincerity. Known for raw, personal lyrics and a willingness to experiment with styles, he has not been afraid to challenge both himself and the industry. This rebellious streak can reflect the Scorpio drive to question norms and explore deeper emotional truths through art. At times, he has clashed with record labels over artistic control, which reveals a strong sense of personal conviction. This readiness to stand by one's principles, even if it causes conflict, echoes the Scorpio trait of standing firm when they believe something is right.

Actress Demi Moore, born November 11, gained fame through various film roles and was one of the highest-paid actresses at one point. Her career has seen ups and downs, yet she keeps moving forward, often reinventing herself. This resilience aligns with Scorpio's association with transformation. Moore's personal life also drew media attention, but she has typically tried to address it on her own terms. Scorpios prefer controlling how much outsiders see, and Moore's approach—sharing some facts but keeping certain matters private—fits this pattern. Her dedication to philanthropic efforts, including supporting charities for children, showcases the caring side that some Scorpios display when moved by a cause.

Actor Stanley Tucci, born on November 11, has also displayed a quiet strength in Hollywood. Famous for roles that vary from comedic to deeply dramatic, Tucci commits himself fully to each character. This consistent excellence, along with a private off-screen life, can demonstrate Scorpio's approach of focusing on substance rather than show. While he is warm in interviews, he rarely shares personal details. Instead, he highlights his passion for cooking or filmmaking. His pivot to hosting food shows and writing cookbooks also reveals a Scorpio-like trait: the ability to channel intense energy into multiple areas. Each new venture shows seriousness and care, hallmarks of Scorpio dedication.

In the literary world, Margaret Atwood, born November 18, is sometimes placed under Scorpio. The author of "The Handmaid's Tale" and many other works, she delves into themes of power, identity, and society's undercurrents. Her storytelling often peels back layers to reveal deeper truths, which can fit Scorpio's tendency to look beneath the surface. Atwood's writing shows a willingness to tackle darker subjects, challenging readers to face uncomfortable realities. She remains measured in interviews, with a witty edge—a style that might match Scorpio's subtlety. Through numerous novels and poems, she has maintained a consistent drive to explore complex questions and encourage critical thinking.

Author and poet Sylvia Plath, born October 27, is also frequently associated with Scorpio. Known for deeply personal works like "The Bell Jar," she bared her emotional struggles in her writing. This raw honesty about inner pain and her intensity in expressing it align with Scorpio's reputation for exploring deep feelings. Sadly, Plath's life ended too soon, but her legacy reveals how a person can channel powerful emotions into art that resonates far beyond their time. While not everyone with a Scorpio birthday experiences life in this same manner, Plath's example highlights the sign's potential for creative expression and emotional depth.

Examining these examples, it is clear that being born under Scorpio does not yield the same life path for each person. Still, many such individuals display tenacity, a capacity for reinvention, and a knack for delving into complex topics—qualities people often link to this sign. Whether they are revolutionizing art, leading scientific breakthroughs, producing deeply moving music, or fighting social battles, they show a blend of passion and focus that stands out. They may also manage their private lives with caution, revealing personal details selectively. Fans who see these patterns may enjoy learning how such traits helped or shaped these famous Scorpios' accomplishments.

It is important to remember that a person's upbringing, environment, and individual choices play big parts in who they become. Astrology offers broad patterns and themes, not strict rules. Some well-known Scorpios might be more open or outgoing than typical descriptions, while others fit the classic mysterious image perfectly. Nonetheless, recognizing certain Scorpio traits in their stories can inspire people who share this sign or who admire these figures. They might notice parallels in their own approach—persistence, emotional depth, or a wish to uncover truth. Seeing how famous individuals overcame hurdles or used their passion can motivate everyday fans to do the same in their personal goals.

CHAPTER 15: COMMON MYTHS ABOUT SCORPIO

Many people have heard claims about Scorpio that paint the sign in an extreme way. These claims often come from magazine horoscopes, social media posts, or brief conversations about astrology. Some label Scorpios as secret villains, others see them as overly dramatic, and some assume they are always angry. These generalizations can be unfair. While Scorpios do have traits like depth and seriousness, they are still individuals with varied personalities. This chapter will look at widespread myths about Scorpio and explain why these ideas are not always correct. By looking more closely, we can see that actual Scorpios are more balanced than rumors suggest.

One common myth is that Scorpios are always mean or harsh. People sometimes believe that a Scorpio will lash out at any moment. This myth arises from Scorpio's ability to defend themselves firmly when they feel threatened. In reality, Scorpio's so-called "mean streak" often appears only when they experience betrayal, repeated dishonesty, or other serious negative behavior. They prefer calm interactions and do not usually look for reasons to attack. If someone treats them with respect and honesty, a Scorpio is unlikely to respond with cruelty. The "mean" image is mostly a misunderstanding of Scorpio's protective approach toward their emotions and loved ones.

Another myth claims that Scorpios never show joy or humor. Some astrological stereotypes suggest they only brood in darkness, never laughing or having fun. This idea overlooks the fact that Scorpios can be quite playful in the right environment. While it is true they might not act silly around strangers, they can have a sharp wit or a clever sense of humor. They sometimes enjoy making quiet jokes that catch others off guard. Friends or family members who see Scorpio's relaxed side know that they can laugh wholeheartedly. The difference is that they share this lighter side selectively, choosing moments when it feels safe and real.

A third myth says Scorpios never forgive and hold grudges forever. It is true that Scorpios can remember when they have been hurt, and they do not let serious betrayals pass without reflection. However, "never forgive" overstates the situation. Many Scorpios work through pain by examining it in private and deciding if they can move on. If the offender shows sincere regret and does not repeat the harmful actions, a Scorpio might gradually rebuild trust. They do not forget the lesson, but they can let go of anger. The idea that they stay angry forever ignores Scorpio's capacity for reflection and growth.

People also claim that all Scorpios are jealous in every situation. This myth arises from stories where a Scorpio becomes suspicious or protective, particularly in love. Yet not every Scorpio acts this way. Jealousy often depends on personal experiences, upbringing, and relationships. Some Scorpios do feel strong emotional reactions if they think a bond is threatened, but this does not mean they act out recklessly. Many Scorpios handle concerns by communicating calmly or by making changes to feel secure. The stereotype of constant, raging jealousy is not accurate. A balanced Scorpio can manage these feelings constructively, especially if they trust the people around them.

Another widespread belief is that Scorpios want to control everyone and everything. While Scorpios like to have a say in matters that affect them, this does not automatically mean they seek full control over others. Their careful nature can be misunderstood as an attempt to dominate. In reality, many Scorpios focus on controlling their own decisions and emotions first. If they see leadership as necessary, they might step in, but they prefer not to micromanage unless they feel it is needed for fairness or proper results. Thus, the idea that all Scorpios are power-hungry overlooks the variety of Scorpio personalities.

Some claim that Scorpios are cold and cannot love. This notion comes from Scorpio's habit of guarding their feelings until they trust someone deeply. They do not always display warmth to strangers. However, once they feel comfortable, Scorpios can show immense devotion, loyalty, and emotional care. Their relationships can be very stable. The outward reserve is a layer of protection, not a lack of feeling. By saying Scorpios cannot love, people miss the point that they actually love very deeply but are careful about where they invest that energy. Seeing them as unfeeling ignores the rich emotional world they often protect.

There is a myth that Scorpio's intensity makes them impossible to be around. In truth, each Scorpio expresses intensity differently. Some channel it into art, research, or solving problems. Others show it by caring for friends, devoting themselves to a hobby, or making big life decisions in a methodical way. Scorpios who manage their strong emotions well can be excellent companions or coworkers. The myth that their intensity is toxic simply lumps together all forms of strong feeling. Properly directed, Scorpio's depth can enhance creative projects, friendships, and team efforts. It is only problematic if combined with harmful habits, which can happen to any sign.

Another misunderstanding is that Scorpios have a mysterious "sixth sense" allowing them to read minds. People notice that some Scorpios appear to guess how others feel, leading to the claim that they have hidden psychic powers. In fact, most Scorpios observe subtle cues—voice changes, facial tics, body language—better than many. Because they are observant, they pick up unspoken signals quickly, creating an illusion of mind-reading. While a few might be more in touch with intuition, it is not magic. It is generally a skilled form of observation that helps them understand people. Labeling it as a mystical gift can lead to unrealistic expectations or confusion.

Some say that Scorpios are always dark, depressed, or fascinated by negative things. While Scorpios do not mind exploring heavier topics—such as life's complexities or deeper questions about human nature—this does not mean they are trapped in sadness. Many Scorpios take an interest in mysteries or serious subjects because they like meaningful discussions. They may enjoy horror movies or detective novels for the excitement of uncovering secrets, not because they glorify negativity. The myth that they are obsessed with gloom overlooks their ability to appreciate beauty, warmth, and everyday contentment. Their attraction to deeper themes is about discovery, not endless sadness.

A related myth is that Scorpios cannot enjoy casual moments or lighthearted events. People think they must constantly investigate or debate serious questions. Although Scorpios do love depth, they can also appreciate simple joys. They might relax by watching a funny show or going for a walk in nature. They often enjoy quiet amusements that let them recharge. The difference is they may not choose loud, chaotic parties or empty small talk. That does not mean they cannot handle simpler moods. They simply prefer to be genuine. Thinking they only want seriousness restricts their diverse range of interests and everyday pleasures.

Another myth contends that Scorpios are naturally untrustworthy. This often arises because Scorpios keep secrets, even about everyday matters. However, holding back personal details does not equal lying. Scorpios may be more private to avoid gossip or to protect their personal world. Once trust is built, a Scorpio can be one of the most reliable allies, keeping confidences others share with them. The idea that they are sneaky or dishonest is a misunderstanding of their reserved style. Of course, any person of any sign can lie, but labeling all Scorpios as untrustworthy misses the point that their private approach is rooted in caution, not deception.

Some myths revolve around Scorpio's element of water. People might say that because they are a water sign, they must be emotional all the time. In practice, each water sign (Cancer, Scorpio, Pisces) handles emotions in distinct ways. Scorpio's approach involves strong feelings combined with a somewhat guarded presentation. This leads some to think they either show no emotion or only dramatic emotion. However, they often experience a range of feelings that they process quietly. The myth that they are either emotionless or hysterical is incorrect. They can find a balanced expression, though it might take time and trust to reveal their inner emotional landscape.

A rumor that persists says that Scorpios sabotage friendships or relationships to test loyalty. This comes from the sign's reputation for wanting proof of devotion. While it is true that some Scorpios test people gently—asking questions or watching actions over time—the idea that they ruin connections on purpose is extreme. Most Scorpios do not plan drama just to see who stays loyal. They are more likely to withdraw or ask direct questions if they have doubts. The notion of grand sabotage is an overblown story. Yes, a Scorpio might walk away from uncertain relationships, but intentionally causing chaos is not typical or universal.

People also claim Scorpios fixate on revenge. Stories circulate about them plotting for years to get even. While a Scorpio might become upset if badly wronged, not all seek revenge. Many do prefer fairness, but they also learn from life experiences. They may choose to move forward quietly rather than engage in fights. If they do decide to confront someone who hurt them, it tends to be because they see no other solution. The myth of Scorpio as a constant avenger exaggerates a real tendency to react strongly when betrayed. In reality, most Scorpios value their time and prefer to invest energy in worthwhile goals rather than endless feuds.

Some mix up Scorpio's curiosity with gossip, assuming they like to dig into everyone's business. In truth, Scorpios do not enjoy shallow rumors. They do have a keen interest in hidden motives or deeper truths, but that is different from gossip. If they sense genuine wrongdoing or secrets that might harm others, they may investigate. But they rarely share this information publicly. Instead, they weigh how it should be handled. The myth that they poke into everyone's life just for entertainment is incorrect. They usually prefer meaningful facts over idle talk. Curiosity and gossip are not the same; Scorpio's curiosity often aims at understanding, not drama.

Another myth says Scorpios lack empathy. Because they do not always display sympathy openly, some assume they do not care about others' feelings. This is not accurate. Many Scorpios are capable of strong compassion; they just show it in subtler ways. Instead of big emotional speeches, they might offer solutions or help behind the scenes. They watch for the right chance to make a difference. If someone is upset, Scorpio might talk with them privately instead of in front of a group. This quieter approach can look detached to those expecting more visible comfort, but it is a form of empathy that values privacy and respect.

Scorpios have been linked to dark magic or secret powers in some folklore, leading to the myth that they are naturally linked to supernatural forces. Stories claim they can curse others just by glaring. These ideas date back to old beliefs where the scorpion creature symbolized danger or hidden threat. However, modern astrology focuses on personality tendencies, not literal magic. A Scorpio may have a mysterious presence or be interested in spiritual topics, but that does not mean they practice dark arts. This myth can create fear or confusion, overshadowing Scorpio's genuine traits, such as a preference for honest interactions and personal boundaries.

A less common but still present myth is that Scorpios cannot work in teams because they hate collaboration. This likely arises from Scorpio's private nature and preference for thorough planning. Yet many Scorpios do well in group settings, especially if the group has clear goals. They might not chat constantly, but they can coordinate tasks, handle research, and provide strategic insights. They only struggle in teams that value shallow conversation or ignore fairness. The claim that they reject collaboration overlooks how often they excel as problem-solvers or planners. A team that respects their focused style can benefit from their skill and determination.

Lastly, some people say Scorpios only care about themselves. This myth arises from misunderstandings of Scorpio's self-protective tendencies. In truth, many Scorpios go to great lengths to support friends, family, or partners once trust is formed. Their loyalty runs deep, and they often sacrifice time or comfort to help someone they love. The assumption that they are purely self-centered is at odds with the caring side observed by close companions. It is more accurate to say they are selective about whom they help. Rather than spread themselves thin, they focus on a few important people or causes, giving genuine support where it matters most.

Seeing these myths laid out, we can understand that each arises from a grain of truth that gets exaggerated. Scorpio does have traits like depth, caution, and emotional power. However, turning these traits into sweeping, negative claims creates unfair stereotypes. Real-life Scorpios vary widely in how they handle feelings, relationships, and personal space. Some are introverts, some are extroverts, and many are somewhere in between. By judging them solely through myths, we miss out on the fact that they can be caring friends, reliable colleagues, and thoughtful family members. Breaking down the myths helps reveal a more balanced view of Scorpio behavior.

Why do these myths persist? One reason is that Scorpio's symbol, the scorpion, has long been associated with danger. People see a scorpion's stinger and assume that those born under Scorpio want to sting others, too. Also, stories of intense or dramatic Scorpios in relationships or media can fuel the flame. Popular culture enjoys extremes—portraying Scorpio as either a perfect mastermind or a vindictive enemy. These images spread easily, turning into simplified statements. Once a myth takes root, it is hard to dislodge, especially if people do not hear from balanced sources. Thus, the myths keep circulating, overshadowing more nuanced facts about Scorpio.

Astrology itself can also contribute to myths if it is presented in shallow ways. Quick horoscopes or memes might focus on "Scorpio is scary" jokes for humor, without explaining the complex sides of the sign. Newcomers to astrology might take these jokes as actual descriptions. Over time, they begin to believe that all Scorpios must be rude, suspicious, or controlling. A better approach is to consult more thorough resources or to speak with real Scorpios, noticing how they behave in practical life. Observing actual behavior rather than relying on headlines can reveal that these negative extremes do not match most Scorpio individuals.

It helps to remember that each zodiac sign has a range of expressions. Not every Scorpio is the same, just as not every Leo or Taurus is the same. Birth charts also include other factors, such as moon signs, rising signs, and planetary placements that shape personality. A Scorpio sun sign might be modified by a gentle moon sign or a flexible rising sign. These combinations can soften or intensify Scorpio traits. Focusing on only the sun sign can create misconceptions. Understanding these variations can debunk myths, showing that while a Scorpio might be intense, they can express it in healthy, balanced ways.

Friends, relatives, and coworkers of Scorpio can help reduce myths by sharing real-life examples. If you know a Scorpio who is kind, loyal, and not at all vengeful, you can challenge someone who claims, "All Scorpios are cruel." Personal stories can be a powerful tool to show that these generalizations are not true. Of course, not every person wants to defend their sign constantly, but occasional clarification can help. Over time, shifting even a few minds can reduce the negative stigma that rests on Scorpio. It encourages a more open-minded approach, where we see individuals for who they are rather than superficial labels.

If you are a Scorpio who faces these myths, it can be frustrating. It might feel like people expect you to act ruthless or suspicious all the time. One response is to calmly explain that you prefer privacy or that you simply take time to build trust. You do not have to argue each myth, but you can show through consistent behavior that you do not fit the extreme images. Over time, those who know you best might become your advocates, correcting others who spread the myths. Your daily actions—being honest, caring, or fair—can speak louder than any rumor about Scorpio character.

In relationships, discussing these myths can be helpful. If a partner or friend believes Scorpio is "always jealous," you can explain how you actually handle jealousy if it arises. Or if they assume you "never forgive," you might share that you do need apologies and clear changes in behavior to move on, but you do not cling to hatred forever. This open conversation helps others see that some beliefs are overblown. It also prevents misunderstandings. Sometimes, people overreact to a small sign of frustration, thinking, "Oh no, the Scorpio rage is coming!" Clarity about your real feelings can avoid such confusion.

If you see negative memes or articles labeling Scorpios as destructive, you can remind yourself that these are exaggerations meant for entertainment. While they can be amusing at times, it is wise not to let them define your sense of self. Recognizing that many comedic takes rely on stereotypes can help you keep perspective. After all, every sign has comedic portrayals—Aries as loud, Virgo as picky, and so on. Using humor to poke fun at these stereotypes can be fun, but problems arise when we take them literally. Knowing the difference between playful jokes and real personality facts can help you stay balanced.

Parents raising Scorpio children can also confront these myths. A parent might worry their Scorpio child will be difficult or moody. While it is true that Scorpio kids can be private or serious at times, they are not necessarily rebellious or mean. Encouraging them to express feelings, giving them some privacy, and respecting their unique traits can foster a healthy sense of self. Teaching them positive ways to handle anger or mistrust can prevent negative patterns. By doing so, a parent helps their Scorpio child avoid feeling forced into the role of the "harsh Scorpio," allowing them to form a confident and well-rounded identity.

Ultimately, these myths about Scorpio grow from a mix of ancient symbolism, scattered observations, and popular culture's love of extremes. The scorpion symbol can look threatening, and some famous Scorpios have displayed intense personalities, which supports the stereotypes. Yet it is crucial to examine individuals more carefully. Not every Scorpio is vengeful, jealous, or obsessed with gloom. Many channel their depth into compassion, creativity, and strong bonds with loved ones. Stepping beyond myths lets us see the more complete picture: a sign that values trust, honesty, and real connections, and that can express passion in thoughtful, caring ways rather than in destructive ones.

Scorpios themselves are aware of these myths, and some might even joke about them. For instance, a Scorpio might laughingly warn a friend not to cross them because "you know, I'm a Scorpio," playing on the stereotype to lighten the mood. In reality, they might be quite gentle. This self-awareness can be a way for Scorpios to manage the awkwardness of those stereotypes. They can disarm people's expectations with humor, showing that they do not take these myths seriously. Over time, consistent positive behavior from real Scorpios can lessen the grip of myths on the public imagination.

Comparing astrology sources can also highlight where myths get repeated. Some older astrology books rely heavily on dramatic language about Scorpio's "dark side," while others provide a more balanced look. Modern astrologers often note that each sign has both positive and negative possibilities. The negativity arises when traits go unchecked or become extreme. For Scorpio, that might be suspicion turning into paranoia or protectiveness turning into manipulation. But balanced Scorpios use their depth to form genuine bonds, their observation skills to handle issues before they worsen, and their resilience to keep going when challenges arise. Recognizing these dual possibilities helps us see beyond the myths.

Encouraging a Scorpio friend or loved one can counter the myths as well. If you see them hesitating to share ideas because they worry about being labeled controlling, reassure them it is okay to speak up. If they fear being seen as vengeful when they express hurt, remind them that healthy communication is the best path forward. By inviting open dialogue, you show that not everyone believes the worst stereotypes. Over time, more people might learn that Scorpios are capable of kindness, warmth, and constructive leadership.

Patience and understanding help replace myths with more accurate, human pictures of how Scorpios behave in day-to-day life.

Myths about Scorpio range from them being cruel to them having supernatural abilities. These exaggerations often ignore the more balanced truth. Real Scorpios display loyalty, depth, and an ability to handle emotions thoughtfully. They do set boundaries and guard their private thoughts, but this does not mean they are evil or withdrawn from the world. By treating each Scorpio as an individual, we see that personality is shaped by experiences, choices, and many aspects of a birth chart. Understanding the real sign behind the myths leads to better connections and less fear. Scorpios, in turn, can share their strong qualities without living under the shadow of harmful stereotypes.

CHAPTER 16: SCORPIO'S FAVORITE ACTIVITIES

Scorpios often choose activities that match their desire for depth and focus. They may enjoy tasks where they can be fully absorbed, whether it is reading, crafting, or exercising. While each Scorpio is unique, this sign generally shows interest in activities that offer meaning, creativity, or a chance to explore something beyond the surface. In this chapter, we will look at a broad range of pastimes and pursuits that Scorpios often gravitate toward. By understanding how these activities align with Scorpio's inner traits, we can appreciate why they find pleasure in anything that sparks curiosity or challenges them to develop their skills further.

One popular area for Scorpios is reading. They might pick up novels with complex plots, deep characters, or even psychological themes. A detective story can be particularly intriguing to them because it involves uncovering secrets. Nonfiction that explains mysteries of science, space, or ancient civilizations might also hold their attention. Rather than skimming a book, they typically read carefully, wanting to absorb details. This kind of focus suits their preference for understanding topics on a deeper level. Quiet reading time also provides the privacy they cherish, allowing them to explore new concepts or stories without interruption or superficial chatter.

Writing is another activity that can draw Scorpio's interest. Whether it is keeping a private journal or composing a short story, writing lets them process their strong emotions and observations. Some Scorpios write poetry or thoughtful blog posts, using words to express what they might not say aloud. The reflective aspect of writing fits their inclination to dive into personal thoughts. They can craft meaningful narratives or share ideas in a way that feels safer than speaking openly. A Scorpio's written work often carries emotional weight, hinting at deeper truths they have observed. This combination of creativity and introspection can be very fulfilling for them.

Many Scorpios have an appreciation for music. They might listen to songs that feature strong lyrics or emotional melodies. Because Scorpio is a water sign tied to feeling, they can be drawn to music that stirs the heart. Some learn to play instruments, such as guitar or piano, channeling their sentiments into performance. They might not be the loudest person on a stage, but they put intensity into each note. The private side of Scorpio could show up as late-night guitar sessions at home or quiet singing sessions where they pour out their soul. Music offers a way for them to connect with themselves and possibly share a bit of their world with others.

Art forms like painting, sketching, or sculpting may appeal to Scorpios who want to create visuals that represent inner feelings. A Scorpio artist might choose rich colors or striking contrasts to convey the intensity of what they sense inside. Even if they do not label themselves as professional artists, they might keep a sketchbook to record ideas or expressions. Some find that shaping clay or using brushes helps them relax after stressful days. This quiet, hands-on activity allows them to transform emotions into tangible pieces. They do not necessarily show these works to everyone, but they value the creative process as a personal release.

Meditative exercises can become a favorite for Scorpios, especially when they need to center themselves. They might explore methods like simple breathing, guided relaxation, or other calming techniques. Because Scorpio can experience strong emotional waves, having a daily or weekly calming practice helps them manage stress or intense thoughts. These calm moments do not have to be long. Even a few minutes of deep breathing can ground them. Some Scorpios incorporate visualization, imagining peaceful scenes to quiet their inner turmoil. Through these activities, they can maintain a healthy balance, channeling their depth into peaceful reflection instead of letting it become overwhelming.

Nature-based activities also hold a special place for many Scorpios. A hike through a dense forest or a walk along a quiet beach can give them time to think, away from the fast pace of daily life. Scorpios appreciate environments where they can observe subtle details—like the sound of leaves underfoot or the pattern of waves. They might not join large hiking groups, preferring a solo or small-group outing. This contact with nature can help them process emotions, find inspiration, or simply feel refreshed. The reflective quality of natural surroundings matches Scorpio's preference for calm introspection alongside meaningful experiences.

Puzzles and strategy games often catch Scorpio's eye. Whether it is a challenging board game, a puzzle box, or a logic puzzle, they love unraveling hidden angles. Mysteries and riddles that test patience and clever thinking align well with Scorpio's investigative streak. They might enjoy escape rooms with friends who also like to solve clues. In quieter settings, they could tackle crosswords, cryptograms, or Sudoku. The mental focus required for these tasks matches Scorpio's willingness to devote time to a single problem. Each solved puzzle brings satisfaction, showing how their determined approach can find answers, even when others might give up.

Scorpios often enjoy physically active hobbies that let them release energy. This can range from martial arts, where discipline and controlled force are important, to activities like swimming, which connects them to the water element. Sports that require strategy or stamina might appeal more than purely showy ones. A Scorpio may pick boxing or kickboxing as a way to train their body and mind together, or they might take up endurance sports like running or cycling. These pursuits allow them to manage stress and channel strong feelings into focus. They do not always talk about these workouts in public, but they can be dedicated behind the scenes.

Cooking or baking can also be a pleasant activity for Scorpios who enjoy creating things that delight senses. They may experiment with recipes involving rich flavors, spicy sauces, or interesting combinations that challenge the palate. Because Scorpios like to uncover secrets, they might research the background of certain dishes or test multiple methods to find the perfect taste. The kitchen can become a quiet laboratory for them, a place where they explore new ideas and get creative. Serving a home-cooked meal to close friends or family might be a subtle way of showing affection, reflecting their willingness to put care into something meaningful.

For those who like technology, Scorpios may try coding or building projects related to computers. Solving tech problems, writing programs, or exploring cybersecurity can feed their curiosity about how systems work. They enjoy understanding the logic behind software or figuring out how to secure information. Technology-based hobbies might include tinkering with hardware or experimenting with new applications. Some find satisfaction in hacking puzzle challenges (in a legal, ethical sense), which involve discovering hidden vulnerabilities. This aligns with Scorpio's love of secrets: they want to see what lies beneath the user interface, learning the deeper structures behind digital tools.

Gardening can be another unexpected favorite for some Scorpios. They might like the symbolic aspect of planting seeds and watching them grow. Tending to plants involves patience and attention, qualities that a dedicated Scorpio can apply. They might research the best soil mixes, lighting conditions, or watering schedules in great detail. Seeing gradual growth can offer them a sense of satisfaction and reflection, as it parallels personal growth. Whether they have a large backyard or a few indoor pots, Scorpio might choose plants with strong or deep colors. A garden, even a small one, can become a peaceful retreat for quiet thought.

Collecting items that hold personal meaning is common among Scorpios. This might involve collecting antiques, vinyl records, or rare books. Part of the attraction is uncovering hidden stories behind each piece. A Scorpio might enjoy searching through old bookstores for a rare edition. Or they could love going to flea markets to find unique objects that speak to them. The process of discovery—looking for clues, inspecting authenticity—can be exciting. These collections often stay private or are only shown to a few trusted friends. Scorpio sees each item as part of a larger narrative that reflects their personal interests and experiences.

Volunteering or supporting causes can also become a favorite activity for some Scorpios, especially if the cause relates to helping people in deeper ways. They might volunteer in crisis centers, wildlife rescue groups, or mentorship programs. Rather than wanting public praise, they tend to serve quietly, contributing consistent effort. The reason they choose these areas is their strong sense of dedication once they believe in something. By focusing on behind-the-scenes tasks—like organizing resources or talking one-on-one with those in need—Scorpio can feel that they are making a real difference. This purposeful involvement matches their drive to bring about meaningful change.

Travel can be compelling for Scorpios, particularly if they can explore historic sites, mysterious ruins, or places with deep cultural backgrounds. They may skip flashy tourist spots, instead heading to locations that hold stories or hidden corners. A Scorpio traveler might enjoy researching folklore or lesser-known attractions. When they arrive, they observe details carefully—architecture, local customs, or the energy of a place. They often keep a travel journal or take photos that capture the mood rather than just the obvious landmarks. Even if they travel with friends, they might slip away at times to soak in the atmosphere on their own.

Scorpios also appreciate group projects that revolve around a common goal, though they prefer smaller groups. They might join a book club focusing on complex literature or a film club analyzing deep plots. These gatherings allow them to exchange thoughts without feeling pressured by large crowds or shallow talk. They can discuss hidden themes in stories or how certain characters show real struggles. The chance to share meaningful perspectives resonates with their love for genuine conversation. A well-structured group can give Scorpio the mental stimulation they enjoy, while also letting them connect with a handful of like-minded people.

Some Scorpios find an outlet in dance or movement, especially if it lets them express intense feelings physically. This could be anything from contemporary dance to more traditional styles. Moving in harmony with music can help them release emotional energy they might hold in. This preference for deeper expression sets them apart from those who just want a carefree dance. Scorpio might treat it like storytelling, focusing on form and mood. Classes or solo practice can both work. When they dance, they are not necessarily showing off for an audience; they may be reflecting on internal emotions and letting them flow through motion.

Films and documentaries draw many Scorpios, especially ones exploring hidden truths, mysteries, or psychological depth. They might watch true crime stories, science documentaries about cosmic mysteries, or thought-provoking dramas. While some shy away from dark themes, Scorpio often wants to see real dilemmas and how people handle them. Discussing the film afterward can be half the fun, dissecting motives or analyzing symbolism. This does not mean they seek negativity. Rather, they are fascinated by the complexity of life. A mind-stirring documentary about wildlife or historical events can spark their curiosity, leading them to do extra research long after the credits roll.

Socially, Scorpios might love cozy gatherings where they can talk openly with a few trusted friends. This could involve game nights, shared meals, or nights spent listening to music together. They do not need a crowd or loud party. Instead, they want real conversations, maybe around a fire pit or a quiet living room. If the group shares a strong bond, Scorpio can be relaxed, showing humor or personal stories. In these small circles, they might propose an interesting group activity—like sharing ghost stories or discussing a recent documentary. This approach combines connection with the depth they naturally enjoy.

In summary, Scorpio's favorite activities often center on depth, meaning, and personal engagement. Whether they are reading, writing, making music, or exploring the world, they look for experiences that allow them to use their intense focus and emotional insight. Many Scorpios crave private moments to recharge, so they often pick hobbies that can be done solo or with a tight-knit group. At the same time, they can shine in collective efforts if the goal resonates with them. From creative pursuits like painting or dancing to intellectual tasks like puzzles or research, their interests mirror the sign's inclination for deeper discovery. Ultimately, these activities let Scorpio channel their powerful energy into growth, art, and thoughtful engagement with life.

CHAPTER 17: SCORPIO WITH OTHER SIGNS

People often like to see how different zodiac signs might relate to each other, and Scorpio is no exception. Each sign in astrology has its own style, so when Scorpio meets another sign, there can be a unique blend of traits. Sometimes there is natural harmony, while other pairings might need patience. This does not mean one sign is better or worse—just that each combination brings different strengths and challenges. In this chapter, we will look at Scorpio's interactions with the other eleven signs, noting common points where they might click and areas they can watch for conflicts. These insights can help friendships, teamwork, or any other group situation.

Scorpio and Aries:

Aries is a fire sign, known for strong energy and a direct manner. Scorpio is water, known for deeper feelings. When these two come together, there can be excitement because both can have fierce determination. Aries might jump into tasks quickly, while Scorpio tends to be more cautious and observe first. This difference can create tension: Aries could see Scorpio as too secretive, and Scorpio might find Aries a bit impulsive. If they respect each other's approaches, they form a powerful team—Aries brings quick action, and Scorpio supplies thoughtful strategy. However, if conflicts arise, both can become stubborn, leading to heated arguments unless they learn to compromise.

Scorpio and Taurus:

Taurus is an earth sign that values stability and comfort. Scorpio, a water sign, can share Taurus's need for loyalty and deep bonds. Both like to form strong connections and can become quite dedicated when they trust each other. The challenge is that each can be stubborn in their own way. Taurus might focus on practical concerns, while Scorpio might focus on emotional truths. When they align, Taurus brings reliable steadiness, and Scorpio adds passion and insight. This can be a supportive pairing in friendships or group work, since they both keep promises. The key is open, honest dialogue so that small disagreements do not turn into bigger problems.

Scorpio and Gemini:

Gemini is an air sign that likes variety and quick changes, while Scorpio prefers deeper focus. Gemini might hop between ideas, enjoying light conversation and new experiences. Scorpio, on the other hand, wants to explore issues in depth, possibly feeling impatient if topics constantly shift. If both learn from each other, Gemini can show Scorpio how to relax or see multiple viewpoints, and Scorpio can show Gemini the importance of looking beneath the surface. In social situations, Gemini might act as the talker, while Scorpio quietly observes. Conflicts may emerge if Gemini sees Scorpio as too secretive, or if Scorpio sees Gemini as too scattered. Good communication helps them find balance.

Scorpio and Cancer:

Cancer is another water sign, so Scorpio and Cancer can share a strong emotional bond. Both can sense each other's moods and appreciate the need for loyalty. Cancer is often caring and focuses on family or close friends, while Scorpio has powerful emotions and a protective streak. Together, they can form a nurturing, secure environment in which both feel safe sharing feelings. Problems can appear if Cancer becomes overly worried, and Scorpio reacts by withdrawing. Talking openly can prevent misunderstandings. When they are at their best, they understand each other's hearts, supporting each other in an almost intuitive way that fosters true closeness.

Scorpio and Leo:

Leo is a fire sign that loves to shine, often enjoying attention. Scorpio can be more private, but also has a commanding presence in quieter ways. This pairing can spark excitement if they admire one another's strengths: Leo's warmth and leadership, and Scorpio's intensity and strong will. However, if Leo wants to dominate the stage without pause, Scorpio might feel overlooked or become resentful. If Scorpio tries to control everything silently, Leo might see it as a threat to their spotlight. Respect and shared admiration can build a powerful partnership. Each can learn from the other: Scorpio might lighten up, while Leo might discover the value of subtle depth.

Scorpio and Virgo:

Virgo is an earth sign that focuses on details and practical steps. Scorpio's water element brings emotional insight, so together they can tackle tasks thoroughly, combining logic and feeling. Virgo might organize schedules or check facts, while Scorpio investigates hidden angles. This can be great for problem-solving, whether at work or in daily life. Conflicts might arise if Virgo becomes too critical, or if Scorpio seems too guarded. However, both typically approach life carefully, so they can bond over shared caution and a respect for facts. Clear and gentle communication can keep them united, allowing them to achieve goals in a calm and purposeful manner.

Scorpio and Libra:

Libra is an air sign known for balance and partnership. They like harmonious interactions and social grace, while Scorpio may prefer deeper, more private connections. If they come together, Libra can smooth out group dynamics, and Scorpio can ensure people do not ignore important underlying issues. This can work well in teamwork or friendships. But if Libra avoids confronting conflicts directly, Scorpio might see that as superficial or evasive. Meanwhile, Libra might find Scorpio's intensity overwhelming. If both sides respect their differences—Libra's wish for peace and Scorpio's focus on truth—this pairing can thrive. They each fill in what the other lacks, making for balanced cooperation.

Scorpio and Scorpio:

When two Scorpios interact, there is a strong sense of mutual understanding. Each recognizes the other's desire for privacy, loyalty, and depth. They can form a bond with unspoken connections, often sensing each other's mood changes before a word is spoken. Problems arise if trust is broken, as both hold onto hurts for a long time. They also have to watch for power struggles: each might want control in subtle ways. However, if they maintain honesty and show mutual respect, this pairing can create a loyal and focused partnership. Their combined determination allows them to tackle big projects or protect those they care about.

Scorpio and Sagittarius:

Sagittarius is a fire sign that values freedom and exploration. They love to share ideas openly. Scorpio, being more private, might initially see Sagittarius as too blunt or restless. Meanwhile, Sagittarius could view Scorpio as intense and secretive. However, there can be excitement in how they encourage each other. Sagittarius might show Scorpio new ways of seeing the world, while

Scorpio can help Sagittarius look at deeper layers instead of just moving on quickly. Challenges appear when Sagittarius's need for open honesty clashes with Scorpio's guarded approach. Finding a balance between honesty and privacy is key. If they manage that, each can grow from the other's perspective.

Scorpio and Capricorn:

Capricorn is an earth sign driven by goals and practicality. Scorpio appreciates Capricorn's steady, hardworking style. Both can value loyalty, responsibility, and achieving something meaningful. In group tasks, Scorpio brings emotional insight, while Capricorn provides structure and planning. They might quietly push each other to succeed and can handle serious challenges together. Problems can come if Capricorn seems too detached or if Scorpio becomes too controlling. Still, they share a serious outlook on life, which can strengthen their bond. When they trust each other, they can accomplish much because they combine a desire for long-term stability with a willingness to address deeper issues.

Scorpio and Aquarius:

Aquarius is an air sign that prizes independent thought and community progress. They often like to brainstorm new ideas or look at issues from unique angles. Scorpio, with a desire for depth, might see Aquarius as sometimes too detached from feelings. Meanwhile, Aquarius could find Scorpio's emotional intensity a bit stifling. On the positive side, Scorpio can help Aquarius focus on personal connections rather than just big picture theories. Aquarius can help Scorpio consider broader social causes and fresh ideas. They may clash if Scorpio tries to hold on too tightly, or if Aquarius ignores Scorpio's need for genuine trust. Respecting each other's styles is important for harmony.

Scorpio and Pisces:

Pisces is another water sign, often gentle, empathetic, and imaginative. Scorpio's strong emotions can harmonize with Pisces's compassionate nature. Both can understand each other's feelings without much need for words. Scorpio's protective side can keep Pisces safe, and Pisces's softness can calm Scorpio's intensity. Problems occur if Pisces becomes too passive or if Scorpio becomes overly controlling. Communication helps them avoid drifting into misunderstandings. Still, there is a natural blend here, since water signs share emotional depth. They can form strong bonds, whether as friends, coworkers, or family members, supporting each other in tough moments and enjoying a sense of mutual empathy.

Given these broad interactions, we see that Scorpio can find common ground with any sign if there is respect, honesty, and understanding of differences. Fire signs might bring excitement but must watch for heated conflicts. Earth signs offer steadiness, though Scorpio should remain open to practical concerns and avoid overprotectiveness. Air signs can expand Scorpio's viewpoints but need to acknowledge Scorpio's preference for depth. Water signs share emotional understanding, yet they must communicate clearly to avoid silent resentments. In any case, each meeting depends on more than just sun signs—people's personalities, life experiences, and communication styles also matter a lot.

When it comes to building friendships, Scorpios often look for loyalty above all else. Signs that respect secrecy and honesty may click faster. A chatty Gemini might still become a close friend to Scorpio if they both appreciate each other's differences and keep trust. Meanwhile, Scorpio can work well with detail-oriented Virgo or goal-driven Capricorn, forming a stable friendship that stands time. The main goal is to allow Scorpio the space to open up at their own pace. People from different signs can be patient, show sincerity, and share interesting discussions. Over time, Scorpios can form lasting bonds regardless of typical sign matches.

In work settings, Scorpio can cooperate with signs that value thoroughness, such as Virgo or Capricorn. Together they can handle large tasks without losing focus. With Aries or Sagittarius, Scorpio might face quick changes, but also get new ideas. Each pairing can be useful if the team respects different styles. If Scorpio is put in a leadership role, they can lead calmly, letting the more energetic signs provide quick action. If another sign is the leader, it is best if they give Scorpio clear tasks and time to think. Working in a fair environment helps Scorpio trust the group, improving teamwork outcomes.

Romantic connections often draw the most attention when discussing sign compatibility. While certain combinations are said to spark quick harmony (like Scorpio and Cancer, or Scorpio and Pisces), any two signs can thrive with mutual effort. Scorpio might enjoy the devotion of a Taurus partner or the emotional link with another water sign. Yet a Scorpio-Leo couple can also bloom if they learn to share the spotlight. Every sign has a different style of expressing affection, so Scorpio's partner should be ready for deep feelings and a need for loyalty. Scorpio, in turn, benefits from being open to the other sign's unique way of caring.

Scorpio can learn from others by appreciating the traits they do not naturally have. For instance, a Scorpio might find that a Libra friend offers guidance on balancing social interactions. A Sagittarian coworker might show how to handle changing conditions without over-worrying. If Scorpio can see these differences as opportunities, they grow. The other signs can also learn from Scorpio's investigative nature and loyalty. By sharing and adopting strengths from each other, signs can form more balanced relationships. This approach reminds us that astrology is about synergy, not judgment—everyone has gifts to share, and each sign can add value to the group.

Still, it is important not to rely too heavily on sign-based assumptions. People vary widely, and many aspects of their birth chart or background can shift how typical "sign matches" play out. A Scorpio with a more flexible rising sign or friendly moon sign might get along better with chatty air signs. Real connections depend on trust, respect, and shared life experiences. A simple label like "fire and water conflict" might overlook common goals or personal efforts. Astrology can hint at dynamics, but real relationships thrive or fail based on how individuals handle problems and show kindness toward each other.

In summary, Scorpio's interactions with other signs revolve around balancing differences and recognizing common ground. Fire signs bring excitement, Earth signs bring stability, Air signs bring broad thinking, and Water signs bring empathy. Each pairing can succeed if there is an effort to combine strengths and respect the potential pitfalls. Scorpio's need for privacy, depth, and loyalty stays constant across all relationships. With understanding and open discussion, Scorpio can form meaningful ties to any sign. This flexible approach highlights that compatibility is not fixed by astrology alone—honesty, compromise, and genuine care help Scorpio and others bridge gaps and build lasting, supportive bonds.

CHAPTER 18: SCORPIO IN DIFFERENT PARTS OF LIFE

Scorpios move through various stages of life just like everyone else, yet their distinctive focus and emotional depth can shape how they approach each phase. From childhood to old age, a Scorpio's traits may become visible in the ways they learn, form relationships, choose careers, and handle responsibilities. Since no two Scorpios are exactly alike, we will look at broad patterns that often arise. By considering typical Scorpio tendencies—privacy, strong will, intense feelings—we can see how they might show up in different parts of life: from early play in childhood to family roles in adulthood, and finally reflections in later years.

Scorpio as a Child:

A Scorpio child might show signs of curiosity early on. They often observe others quietly, possibly playing on their own while watching the room. Even as toddlers, they might pick up on emotional undercurrents at home. If there is tension or conflict, they sense it quickly, even if the adults do not spell it out. While they can be caring, they also have a strong will. If they want to do something in their own way, they might resist being forced or tricked. Parents can help by respecting the child's need for some privacy, while also teaching them positive ways to express frustration or hurt.

At preschool or elementary age, Scorpio kids could be the ones asking "why" a lot, but in a quieter style. They might not always raise their hand in class, but they go home thinking about the topics. These children sometimes form close bonds with one or two good friends rather than a large group. Loyalty matters to them even at this young age. If a friend betrays their trust, they can react with tears, anger, or going silent. Handling these strong feelings is part of their early growth. Encouraging them to talk about what bothers them can teach them that healthy communication eases misunderstandings.

Scorpio in the Teenage Years:
During adolescence, Scorpio traits can intensify because teens are already dealing with new emotions and social pressures. A Scorpio teen might keep secrets or personal diaries, exploring thoughts they do not share. They could have a strong sense of fairness and might call out dishonesty among peers. While they can show fierce loyalty to close friends, they may also test bonds if they worry someone is not genuine. Teen Scorpios might explore creative outlets like writing or music to handle strong emotions. Adults in their life can help by giving them space to reflect but also encouraging them to speak openly when they feel overwhelmed or misunderstood.

At school, a Scorpio teen may excel in subjects that require investigation or critical thinking—like science, history, or literature. They enjoy digging into details, forming theories, or uncovering hidden themes in stories. Group projects can be interesting: they might work hard but expect others to do their share. If someone is lazy, Scorpio could call them out or silently decide not to trust them again. Friendships can run deep, but drama might arise if trust is broken. Overall, by the end of the teenage years, a Scorpio often has a clearer sense of who they are, shaped by experiences that tested their loyalty and resilience.

Scorpio as a Young Adult:

Entering early adulthood, Scorpio might focus on goals with seriousness. Whether they attend college, join the workforce, or learn a trade, they often put intense effort into chosen paths. Their sense of privacy remains, so classmates or coworkers might only see part of their personality. Scorpio may choose a few close allies in these environments, forming small but strong social circles. In romantic or deeper friendships, they begin to refine what they want from relationships. They do not mind waiting for a partner who respects their boundaries and shares their dedication to trust. This time also sees them testing potential careers, seeking roles that allow thorough engagement.

Financially, young adult Scorpios might handle money carefully, either saving for long-term security or researching investments with a detective-like approach. If they discover something that feels right, they commit. They dislike being rushed and prefer to study all angles first. Some Scorpios might even explore business ownership or freelance work to maintain control over projects. In social events, they might skip large parties in favor of meaningful gatherings. Over these years, they learn to balance independence with collaboration—whether that involves roommates, coworkers, or personal ventures. This stage sets the foundation for their future, where Scorpio can refine their ambitions and personal style.

Scorpio in Career Development:

As Scorpio progresses in work life, their deep focus often becomes a valuable asset. They might specialize in fields like research, finance, medicine, psychology, investigation, engineering, or any area requiring careful thought. If they feel passionate about a field, they commit fully, sometimes rising to leadership roles. They might keep a calm exterior in stressful moments, leading teams through tough challenges. If they do not trust the company's ethics, they might leave or speak out. Scorpio values moral integrity. Over time, they build a reputation for thoroughness and reliability. Their coworkers learn that once they trust you, they are steady, but if that trust is lost, it is tough to rebuild.

In the office, Scorpio might prefer smaller teams or projects where they have some control. They tend to avoid open conflict but can be direct when needed. If they see a hidden problem, they bring it up calmly, backing it with facts. Others might be surprised by how much Scorpio observes. While promotions may come from their consistent performance, Scorpio does not always advertise achievements loudly. They rely on results to speak for them. Mentoring can also appear: some Scorpios enjoy guiding new hires, sharing knowledge in a quiet but supportive way. This leads to a workplace environment where people can grow if they respect Scorpio's no-nonsense approach.

Scorpio and Family Life (Adulthood):

In creating a home, Scorpio might aim for a space that feels private and comfortable, favoring colors or styles that match their preference for calm. If they choose to raise children, they can be protective and devoted, teaching the kids about honesty and loyalty. However, they also need to watch for being too strict. By offering gentle support and open communication, they help children feel safe enough to share problems without fear. A Scorpio parent might quietly handle many details behind the scenes—managing finances, planning for emergencies—so the family stays secure. They find pride in keeping loved ones well-cared for, even if they do not show off about it.

Marriages or long-term partnerships for Scorpio often hinge on mutual trust. Scorpio invests deeply in a partner they believe in, but if they sense betrayal, strong conflicts can follow. When trust endures, they can form stable, supportive units. Some Scorpios enjoy hosting small family gatherings or close friend get-togethers, but they might not invite large groups often. Instead, they treasure intimate dinners where real conversations happen. Day by day, Scorpio's family approach leans on consistent loyalty rather than big speeches. Partners and children might learn that even if Scorpio does not speak constantly about feelings, their quiet actions show deep care and dedication.

Scorpio in Community Involvement:

Outside the home, Scorpio might choose specific community causes to support, especially if they see a hidden or overlooked issue. They might volunteer for crisis centers, animal rescue, or local policy groups. When they give time, they do it seriously, researching facts and ensuring help is actually reaching people. They do not usually volunteer just for socializing. Instead, they want the effort to matter. If they see corruption or dishonesty in the organization, they may expose it or leave. Their protective instincts can also guide them to stand up for neighbors or friends facing unfairness. Over the years, they earn trust among those who appreciate thorough, behind-the-scenes workers.

Scorpio in Midlife:

As they enter middle age, Scorpios often reflect on what they have achieved and whether they are living according to their inner principles. Some might make big changes, leaving careers that no longer feel meaningful or shifting family routines if they see problems. They rely on their accumulated wisdom, not just gut feelings, analyzing patterns that have played out for decades. Friendships at this stage can be well-established, consisting of people who proved trustworthy. Scorpio might also pick up new interests or deeper studies, like a new language or advanced training in a hobby, because they never lose that investigative spark. This period can bring personal growth if they stay open-minded.

In health, middle-aged Scorpios might double down on routines that maintain strength—regular exercise, balanced meals, and mental wellness practices. They recognize their stress levels can get high if they do not manage them. By this age, they likely have methods for calming themselves, such as meditative exercises, quiet reading, or solitary walks. Some may find a renewed interest in creative arts they loved as children or teenagers. This helps them express bottled-up feelings in a constructive way. They might also become mentors to younger colleagues or to nieces and nephews, passing on insights about loyalty, determination, and facing life's difficulties with resolve.

Scorpio in Later Life (Senior Years):

In older age, Scorpios may embrace a calmer pace while still maintaining a sharp mind. They can be the wise family member or community elder who notices details others overlook. Their recollections of events carry emotional depth, so younger folks might learn from their stories. They sometimes choose peaceful pastimes—like gardening, writing memoirs, or collecting historical facts—and find comfort in reviewing life lessons. While they might not crave large social events, they enjoy visits with loyal friends and family. If health challenges arise, they approach them with quiet determination, wanting to understand treatments and protect their dignity as best they can.

Older Scorpios often reflect on relationships they built over the years. If they have strong bonds with children or grandchildren, they can offer support or guidance behind the scenes. They prefer heart-to-heart talks over superficial chitchat. Because of their careful observation, they can spot which younger relatives need encouragement. They might step in, giving practical help or advice. Some Scorpios at this stage also engage in spiritual or philosophical explorations, pondering life's meaning. They might read about different beliefs, compare ideas, and form personal conclusions. Their open but thoughtful approach can become a source of quiet inspiration for those around them.

Throughout all parts of life, Scorpios might encounter challenges related to trust. Friendships can grow deeply if trust is honored, or fall apart if betrayal occurs. In the career realm, they succeed best where they can focus and maintain ethical standards. As family members, they thrive by balancing protectiveness with empathy for each person's individuality. Hobbies that allow for exploration—be it puzzle-solving or emotional expression—make them feel fulfilled. Even in later years, they look for meaningful involvement, whether mentoring or volunteering. The same themes appear again and again: privacy, loyalty, emotional understanding, and a quest to ensure that what they do has genuine worth.

Scorpios also learn that too much secrecy can cause tension. In childhood or teen years, hiding worries might lead parents or teachers to misunderstand them. As adults, not sharing vital information with friends or partners can create unnecessary distance. Over time, many Scorpios learn that selective honesty can bring people closer without losing privacy. Another life skill is handling anger or hurt feelings. Holding onto grudges can hinder personal development. Thus, finding healthy outlets—talking with trusted people, writing, or creative arts—helps them let go. The more Scorpios manage these strong emotions in positive ways, the better they adapt across all stages.

It also helps if Scorpios recognize that not everyone picks up on unspoken signals as easily as they do. In early life, they might expect friends or family to notice subtle hints. If that does not happen, misunderstandings can arise. As they mature, they often learn to communicate needs more directly. Similarly, some tasks require collaboration even if Scorpio prefers independence. For example, a group project might be stronger if they share ideas before finalizing them alone. Gaining these communication skills and cooperative habits can open more doors. Then, whether at 20 or 70, Scorpios can connect with the right people while keeping healthy boundaries.

CHAPTER 19: TIPS FOR SCORPIO

Many Scorpios appreciate guidance that respects their private nature. They might not want loud advice, but they can benefit from hints and practical steps that let them handle life's daily challenges more smoothly. Here, we will look at simple tips that can help a Scorpio make the most of their strong feelings and sharp mind. These ideas address everything from handling stress to forming reliable friendships. By taking small, steady steps, Scorpios can stay focused on their aims, keep their emotional balance, and work well with others. While each Scorpio is different, these general pointers can serve as a starting point for positive growth.

Tip 1: Honor Your Need for Solitude

Scorpios often need personal time to think and calm down. If your schedule is very busy, try to carve out at least a few minutes each day to be alone—whether it is sitting quietly, taking a short walk, or reading in your favorite chair. This habit can keep stress under control. If you live with family or roommates, explain that these quiet moments help you stay balanced. You do not have to share every detail of how you feel, but a simple mention—"I need a little private time now"—can lead to better understanding. Over time, these short breaks can recharge your emotional and mental energy.

Tip 2: Practice Direct Communication

Scorpios sometimes assume others notice the same small signs they do, but not everyone has your level of observation. If a friend or family member overlooks your signals that you feel upset, try stating it kindly: "I am worried about this," or "I feel left out." This direct approach can prevent confusion. It does not mean you must share all your secrets; it just ensures that small misunderstandings do not grow. Being honest about a problem early can save you from deeper hurt later on. Use a calm tone, showing that you seek solutions, not conflict. This can help others respond in a supportive way.

Tip 3: Channel Strong Emotions into Safe Outlets

Your feelings can run deep. If you sense anger or sadness building, find an activity that eases the weight. It might be writing, painting, playing music, or doing a physical workout. These outlets let you express tension without harming relationships. For example, if you had a stressful day at school or work, spend some time journaling your thoughts. If writing is not your style, try moving your body—like taking a brisk walk or doing stretches while listening to music. This can prevent you from bottling up intense emotions. Over time, you will see that releasing feelings in healthy ways keeps you calmer and stronger.

Tip 4: Set Clear Boundaries but Allow Some Flexibility

Scorpios do well when they define personal lines—like not letting casual acquaintances know all your private matters. These boundaries protect you from gossip or betrayal. At the same time, be careful not to keep walls so high that new friends cannot approach you. Allow yourself to loosen some boundaries with people who have shown consistent honesty and kindness. Gradually sharing bits of yourself can deepen trust. True, you might face disappointments, but a balanced approach can lead to rewarding connections. Knowing how to adjust boundaries based on the situation helps you manage trust wisely while still building meaningful bonds over time.

Tip 5: Recognize When Perfectionism Hinders You

You can be very thorough, double-checking details that others overlook. While this skill is valuable, it can morph into perfectionism if you are not careful. Be kind to yourself when tasks do not go exactly as planned. Ask, "Is this detail truly essential, or am I stuck?" Sometimes, stepping back to see the bigger picture helps you realize that minor mistakes will not ruin the entire project. Giving yourself permission to do your best, rather than demanding perfection, lowers stress. This also makes you more flexible with others, who might not hold the same exacting standards but still want to help the team succeed.

Tip 6: Build Emotional Awareness

Scorpios can be so private that they even hide feelings from themselves. Periodically check how you feel: anxious, excited, weary, or sad. Naming the emotion can reduce its intensity. If you find it hard to label your mood, consider writing short notes each day, like "Felt annoyed in the morning when…," or "Felt proud after finishing…." Over time, patterns appear—maybe you get stressed in crowded places or become happiest after finishing a project. Identifying these triggers allows you to plan better. If certain tasks upset you, you can prepare coping methods. By staying in touch with your emotions, you also become better at communicating needs to friends or coworkers.

Tip 7: Learn to Forgive for Your Own Well-Being

It is true that Scorpios remember betrayals and can hold onto anger. Yet holding onto old hurts can weigh you down more than it impacts the other person. Forgiving does not mean you must forget the lesson or welcome the betrayer back into close friendship. It simply means releasing the tight hold anger has on you. You might set new boundaries with that person or end the relationship if trust is gone.

But letting go of the grudge frees mental energy you can use for healthier goals. Think of it as clearing out emotional clutter. A counselor or supportive friend can help you navigate forgiveness at your own pace.

Tip 8: Use Your Observation Skills Kindly

Scorpios are often gifted at noticing small changes in body language, tone, or atmosphere. While you can use these insights to protect yourself, also consider how you can help others. If you see a friend acting nervous, gently check in: "You seem off today—want to talk?" This can build deeper bonds. Avoid turning your keen observation into suspicion about everyone. Instead, treat it as a valuable tool to understand what is beneath the surface. If you do sense a genuine problem, bring it up respectfully. Others may be grateful that you noticed. This supportive approach can transform your watchfulness into a social strength.

Tip 9: Accept Compliments and Praise

It is common for Scorpios to sidestep public attention. If someone praises your effort—at work, in school, or among friends—try not to brush it off. While you do not have to boast, a simple "Thank you" acknowledges their kind words. This can strengthen relationships because people see that you value their recognition. If you repeatedly dismiss compliments, folks may feel uncertain about approaching you. Allow yourself to feel proud of your hard work without worrying you are showing off. This can boost your confidence and help you realize that your quiet style does not mean you must hide achievements or avoid all positive attention.

Tip 10: Keep an Eye on Jealousy

When you care deeply, you sometimes worry about losing those you value. A spark of jealousy might flare if you think someone is threatening a close bond. Recognize that occasional jealousy is normal, but do not let it drive your actions. Instead of jumping to conclusions, gather facts or calmly talk with the person involved. Perhaps you misread a situation, or maybe there is a simple explanation. If the issue is real, handle it with honest dialogue instead of silent resentment. Overcoming jealousy involves trusting your own worth and the loyalty of those who have shown they genuinely respect you.

Tip 11: Practice Saying "I Need Help"

Scorpios pride themselves on being capable and self-reliant, which can be an asset in problem-solving. Yet there are times when reaching out to others can lighten your load. Asking for help is not weakness; it is a shared human experience. If you face a tough assignment, talk with a teacher or coworker for guidance. If you feel emotional stress, consider confiding in a trusted friend, family member, or mental health professional. This does not reduce your autonomy; instead, it shows you respect your well-being. Over time, you will notice that others appreciate the chance to support you, and bonds of trust grow stronger.

Tip 12: Explore Healthy Activities that Match Your Depth

Not everyone wants to chat about mysteries or read books on psychology. If you love deeper themes, look for clubs, forums, or events where like-minded people gather. This could be a local book club that explores serious novels, a documentary group, or an online forum discussing space science or history. Engaging with people who share your interests can reduce feelings of being misunderstood. It also provides a safe outlet for the heavier discussions you enjoy. While casual topics have their place, fulfilling your desire for substance in a supportive setting can feed your mind and emotions in a healthy way.

Tip 13: Keep Learning About Trust

Trust is a major theme for Scorpios, and you might refine how you handle it over the years. Notice that trust is not all-or-nothing. It can be built in stages. If a new coworker is friendly, you can share a small piece of information and watch how they handle it. If they respect your privacy, you can share a bit more next time. This gradual approach helps you avoid giving too much to the wrong person. Also, realize that mistakes happen. A friend might slip up. Evaluate if it was malicious or a minor accident. Differentiating between serious betrayal and human error helps maintain balanced relationships.

Tip 14: Balance Introspection with External Feedback

Your reflective nature means you spend a lot of time in your own thoughts. This can foster self-awareness but might lead to overthinking if you never get outside opinions. Consider sharing your concerns or decisions with a trusted confidant. Hearing another viewpoint can reveal blind spots or ease worries you have amplified in your mind. Of course, pick someone you know is fair and respects your boundaries. Even if you do not follow their suggestions, simply hearing different angles can sharpen your thinking. You remain in control of your decisions, but you gain the benefit of stepping outside your inner echo chamber.

Tip 15: Celebrate Small Wins (in Your Own Way)

While you might not want a big party for every achievement, it is healthy to recognize progress. This can be as simple as telling yourself, "I did well today," or treating yourself to something you enjoy—like a nice cup of tea or a new book. Such small acknowledgments help you stay motivated and remind you that every step counts toward bigger goals. You do not have to post about it or share with everyone, but do not completely ignore your efforts. A private sense of pride can boost self-esteem. This approach also encourages you to keep striving without the burden of needing public attention.

Tip 16: Embrace Calm Conflict Resolution

In disagreements, your firm stance can be useful, but watch out for letting anger simmer. Address conflicts directly while they are small. If a situation upsets you, pick a calm moment to discuss it with the other person. Explain what bothered you and why. Then, listen to their perspective. This helps prevent grudges. If the conversation becomes too heated, suggest a break and resume later. Try not to bring up old issues unless they directly connect to the current problem. Learning to solve conflicts without building long-term resentment can make your friendships or relationships stronger and more stable over time.

Tip 17: Allow Yourself to Change

As a fixed sign, Scorpio likes consistency, but life involves growth. You are allowed to shift opinions, adapt habits, or approach old problems in new ways. Do not feel forced to stick to an outdated stance just because you once defended it. If fresh information arises, use your strong mind to reassess. This does not mean you are weak. It shows you are mature enough to integrate new facts. For example, if you used to ignore a friend's hobby but discover it has deeper value, you might develop an interest. Embracing these changes can keep your life fresh and your mind open.

Tip 18: Reach Out to Kindred Spirits

Sometimes, being a Scorpio can feel isolating if you are surrounded by people who only engage in surface-level talk. Finding even one person who shares your hunger for honesty or your fascination with deeper subjects can make daily life more rewarding. This might be a teacher, mentor, colleague, or friend. Start conversations about topics you love or look for local groups. By creating a network of supportive folks, you gain a sense of acceptance without having to reveal everything to everyone. It is not about quantity, but quality. Even a small circle of true connections can help you thrive socially and emotionally.

Tip 19: Use Compassion Toward Yourself and Others

Scorpios can be very tough on themselves when goals are not met. Remember to treat yourself with the same kindness you might show a close friend. If you see a friend or sibling struggling, extend understanding rather than silent judgment. Your empathy can help them feel safer opening up. Doing so also reminds you that mistakes are part of being human. By practicing compassion, you soften tension in daily life, making it easier to handle stress and disappointment. This approach does not weaken your boundaries or seriousness; it simply balances your powerful determination with a gentle side that fosters better relationships.

Tip 20: Reflect on Your Progress Regularly

Set aside time—maybe monthly or every few months—to think about what is working in your life and what is not. Ask yourself: "Am I building trust with the right people?" "Have I been fair in my reactions?" "What new challenges am I ready to explore?" Writing these reflections in a journal or talking them over with a trusted friend can keep you aware of your patterns. This helps you avoid drifting into old habits like holding grudges or hiding emotions too much. By staying actively engaged in your own growth, you make sure your strong focus leads you forward, rather than keeping you stuck.

Tip 21: Balance Your Protective Instinct

Your loyalty to family and close friends can be strong, and that is admirable. But be cautious about going overboard. Sometimes, loved ones must solve problems on their own. If you try to shield them from every difficulty, you might rob them of the chance to learn and grow. Before stepping in, ask if they truly want help. This approach respects their independence while still honoring your caring side. Similarly, be open to them helping you if you are in need. A balanced dynamic—where you both protect each other without smothering—can keep relationships healthy, ensuring everyone benefits from your devoted nature.

Tip 22: Find Professional Support if Needed

Because Scorpios can be so private, it may be hard to consider therapy or counseling. However, if you feel overwhelmed by anxiety, grief, or unresolved conflicts, talking to a trained professional can help. They keep what you say confidential, giving you a safe environment to explore feelings. This does not mean you have to reveal all secrets instantly. You can take time to build trust, just as you would in any relationship. Over time, a counselor can guide you in handling intense emotions more effectively. If therapy seems uncomfortable, you might try anonymous hotlines or support groups that address specific issues.

Tip 23: Appreciate Your Positive Traits

You possess strong willpower, depth, and a sense of loyalty that is rare. Recognize the good in these qualities. Yes, every trait can go too far if misused, but your commitment and emotional insight can be real superpowers in daily life. You might solve problems others find too complicated, or offer real empathy to a friend in crisis. At work, your thoroughness can prevent mistakes. In personal relationships, your sincerity fosters deep trust. Sometimes, you might get too focused on the negative myths about Scorpio. Remind yourself that with balanced handling, your traits can shine in a way that benefits both you and those around you.

Tip 24: Embrace Humor and Lightness When Possible

Your natural inclination for seriousness can cause you to overlook small, amusing moments. Try to notice the funny side of daily happenings. Maybe a coworker tells a silly joke, or a friend sends a lighthearted message. Let yourself enjoy these brief breaks from heavy thoughts. Laughter reduces stress and helps you connect with people who might not share your depth but still appreciate a simple, friendly bond. You do not have to become a comedian or hide your seriousness, but acknowledging everyday humor can keep your emotional range flexible. It also encourages others to see that while you value depth, you are not always intense.

Tip 25: Remain Open to Feedback in Work and Relationships

When someone offers suggestions on your performance—be it a manager, mentor, teacher, or friend—try to listen calmly. If they speak from a place of care, their comments could reveal ways you can grow. It is natural to feel defensive, but ask questions to clarify what they mean. Maybe you can apply their advice to enhance your work or approach conflicts differently. This does not mean you have to accept every critique. You can still weigh if it fits your principles. However, staying open-minded helps you catch improvements you might otherwise miss. By doing so, you cultivate ongoing progress without compromising your integrity.

Tip 26: Clarify Intentions When Things Are Confusing

If you suspect a friend or coworker is acting oddly but are not sure why, do not jump straight to worst-case scenarios. Politely ask them what is going on. Sometimes, they might just be tired or stressed.

Direct, calm questioning can spare you from spending hours worrying. Likewise, if you see conflict brewing within a group, speak up. "I sense some tension—anything I can help with?" This proactive style allows your investigative nature to be helpful instead of purely suspicious. People might open up, and you might solve a small problem before it balloons. This fosters a healthier environment at home or work.

Tip 27: Observe But Avoid Over-Interpreting

Your natural gift for reading subtle signals is a plus, but be aware that you might read too much into things. For instance, if a friend replies briefly to your text, it might be because they are busy, not because they are annoyed with you. Practice checking facts. A quick, direct question—"All good?"—can clear confusion. Not every short response or distant look means someone is hiding betrayal. Give yourself room to interpret carefully, but also accept simpler explanations. This balance keeps your analytical nature from turning into worry or mistrust. Over time, you will refine your sense of when your gut feelings are truly accurate.

Tip 28: Celebrate Your Milestones with Those You Trust

When you reach an important goal—finishing a tough project, overcoming a fear, or making progress in personal health—mark the moment with your inner circle. You do not need a grand event. A quiet meal or a small token of recognition can suffice. Doing so reassures friends or family that you enjoy their company and that you value shared happiness. It also reminds you that support can be mutual, not one-sided. People close to you want to see your success. By letting them in, you strengthen those bonds. This approach avoids public fanfare but still honors your achievements in a comfortable, private manner.

Tip 29: Remember Life Is Not Always Hidden

Though you enjoy uncovering hidden layers and solving puzzles, not every situation or person carries a deep mystery. Sometimes things are just what they seem. If you find yourself overcomplicating a simple matter, pause and consider the straightforward explanation. This can save energy and keep your mind from going in circles. By accepting that some areas of life are plain and do not require deep probing, you can reserve your investigative strengths for bigger goals or genuine puzzles. This does not mean losing your sense of depth—it means focusing it where it truly matters, rather than scattering it on everyday trivial events.

Tip 30: Stay Flexible in Team Settings

Scorpios often excel in tasks that let them concentrate alone. However, you will sometimes face group work—whether in school or at a job. Try to compromise on small details. For instance, if a teammate insists on a certain format for a presentation, weigh whether it truly harms the final outcome. If it does not, be flexible. Reserve your firm stance for bigger issues, such as honesty or thoroughness. This method prevents friction. Also, share credit fairly, acknowledging each person's effort. Doing so builds trust, showing you are not just protective of your own interests. Over time, you might find group projects more productive and less stressful.

Tip 31: Maintain a Supportive Environment

Your home or personal space can affect your mood. If possible, arrange it to suit your preference for calm and privacy. This might mean keeping clutter to a minimum or choosing subdued lighting. You might also enjoy relaxing scents like lavender or sandalwood. Creating a peaceful atmosphere can keep your mind from feeling crowded. If you live with others, find a small corner you can call your own—maybe a desk or a reading nook. This environment supports your need to focus or recharge after a busy day. Tending to your surroundings helps balance your intense inner world with a sense of outer stability.

Tip 32: Embrace Opportunities to Laugh with Friends

Even if you prefer serious discussions, do not shy away from spontaneous fun. If a friend suggests a simple game or a silly outing, consider joining. You might discover a refreshing lightness that relieves stress. Sharing laughter builds trust in another way: it shows you are comfortable enough to let your guard down. This does not conflict with your deeper interests. You can have both silly shared moments and serious talks in the same friendship. Also, sometimes laughter can lead to better problem-solving by releasing tension. So, let yourself enjoy these opportunities to connect in a carefree manner now and then.

Tip 33: Keep Realistic Expectations in Romance

If you are in a romantic relationship or seeking one, remember that no partner can read minds all the time, even if you are good at sensing unspoken cues. Communicate what matters to you—such as honesty, loyalty, and meaningful conversation. At the same time, ask about your partner's needs too. Mutual effort is essential. It is normal to have small clashes, so do not interpret every dispute as betrayal. Learn to differentiate everyday disagreements from real breaches of trust. By keeping expectations grounded and using open communication, you can form a stable bond that respects each person's individuality while sharing mutual care.

Tip 34: Develop a Personal Relaxation Practice

Strong emotions sometimes build up quickly for Scorpios, so having a go-to method for relaxation is crucial. This can be breathing exercises, listening to calm music, or spending time with a pet. Some

Scorpios enjoy guided imagery—closing their eyes and picturing a peaceful place. Others prefer gentle movement, like yoga or slow stretching. Consistency is key: doing it only once might not help as much as having a regular routine. By integrating relaxation into daily life, you reduce the chance of sudden outbursts or silent brooding. Over time, you will notice your stress levels drop, letting your natural strengths shine more clearly.

Tip 35: Find Mentors You Trust

Whether you are a student, a rising professional, or well into your career, having a mentor can open new paths. Look for someone whose ethics you admire and who shares knowledge willingly. Since Scorpios value loyalty and privacy, choose a mentor who respects personal boundaries. Ask for guidance on specific skills or decisions. Mentors can provide a broader view, spotting chances for you to apply your strengths. Over time, this relationship can grow into a supportive connection where you learn advanced methods while maintaining your independent style. A good mentor does not force you to reveal everything but offers insight you might otherwise miss.

Tip 36: Distinguish Authentic Warnings from Unfounded Worries

Scorpios often get "gut feelings" when something seems off. This can be a real talent, saving you from bad deals or dishonest people. But sometimes, normal stress or small misunderstandings can trigger your internal alarm unnecessarily. Before acting, gather facts. Consider writing down your concern: "This person's behavior changed—possible reasons?" Evaluate if it is truly suspicious or if they might be dealing with unrelated stress. This method ensures that you use your intuition wisely rather than letting it run wild. Over time, by comparing your initial impressions with real outcomes, you refine your sense of genuine warnings versus everyday quirks in life.

Tip 37: Offer Support Without Expecting Perfect Reactions

When friends or family have problems, you might jump in with solutions or protective measures. This can be caring, but remember that they might not react exactly as you expect. Some people need time before accepting help. Others might do the opposite of your advice. Resist feeling personally offended if they do not follow your suggestions. Your role is to present options, not to guarantee they will act on them. By letting them find their own path—while still offering a listening ear—you show respect. This approach preserves your helpful spirit yet avoids controlling their choices, leading to healthier, more balanced relationships.

Tip 38: Plan for the Future While Staying Flexible

Scorpios generally like having clear goals. You might set a long-term plan for career, family, or personal growth. This can be a strong motivator. However, life can change directions. Being flexible enough to update your plan does not mean you failed; it shows adaptability. If a new opportunity appears that aligns with your deeper purpose, consider adjusting. If external events force you to change course, give yourself permission to pivot without feeling you abandoned your path. Keep the core of your aims—such as living with honesty or helping others—intact, but adapt the details to fit current realities. This way, your strong will stays productive.

Tip 39: Practice Gratitude for Emotional Balance

Sometimes, focusing on what is missing or who might betray you can overshadow life's positives. Combat this by listing things you appreciate—like a supportive friend, a nice meal, or a small success at work. This does not require you to ignore genuine problems. Instead, it balances your viewpoint. By regularly reminding yourself of small good aspects, you keep from drowning in suspicion or worry. This simple practice can calm anxious thoughts, making it easier to handle deeper tasks. Whether you keep a gratitude journal or mentally note items each day, these small acknowledgments can brighten your mood and reinforce hope.

Tip 40: Recognize the Difference Between Privacy and Isolation

Privacy means choosing whom you trust, but isolation is cutting yourself off from everyone. Periods of alone time can be refreshing, yet if you find you are always avoiding gatherings or never sharing anything personal, you may be sliding into isolation. Ask if you feel lonely or if you truly prefer the activity on your own. If it is loneliness, consider reaching out to a friend, even if just with a short message. Overcoming complete isolation in small steps can help keep you socially healthy. Stay aware that letting in a bit of companionship does not threaten your sense of self or your personal boundaries.

By applying these tips, you can leverage the best parts of being a Scorpio—focus, loyalty, emotional insight—while reducing potential pitfalls like extreme secrecy, grudge-holding, or suspicion. Remember that personal growth is an ongoing process, and you do not need to change everything overnight. Pick one or two ideas from this list and see how they fit into your life. Over time, you can build on successes, adjusting methods to suit your particular style. Through patience and reflection, you will find ways to manage intense feelings and build strong relationships. Embracing these strategies can help you move forward with more confidence, security, and a sense of balance.

CHAPTER 20: FINAL THOUGHTS ON SCORPIO

Scorpio is a sign that many people view with a mix of curiosity and respect. Across the chapters, we have looked at Scorpio's foundation—ranging from personality traits and emotional depth to history, myths, and day-to-day habits. We have also explored how Scorpios might connect with other signs and handle relationships in families, friendships, and workplaces. Now, let us bring everything together in these final thoughts. The Scorpio sign can offer remarkable loyalty and focus, yet it faces challenges around trust and intense feelings. Understanding these features helps both Scorpios and those close to them navigate interactions in a more supportive, thoughtful way.

One of Scorpio's standout traits is its strong will. When a Scorpio decides to learn a skill or achieve a certain goal, they often push forward with determination that impresses others. This can be seen in a student who masters a subject few others tackle, or in an employee who solves tough problems at work. While people admire this persistence, it can also backfire if Scorpio remains fixated on a plan that no longer serves them. Knowing when to pivot or accept new information is vital. The ability to combine perseverance with adaptability can make Scorpio more effective in almost any role they choose.

Another core aspect is emotional depth. Scorpios are not simply moody; they sense layers of feelings in themselves and others. This can lead to empathy, especially when they see someone in genuine pain. They might be the friend who listens quietly, catching cues that others might miss. But deep feelings can also overwhelm if not managed. Scorpios who learn healthy methods to handle anger, jealousy, or sorrow often avoid the pitfalls of letting these emotions fester. On the flip side, those who deny or hide their feelings for too long might experience sudden outbursts or withdraw from friends without explaining why.

Trust runs through Scorpio's life like a guiding thread. They want bonds where honesty and loyalty are non-negotiable. This can lead to incredibly strong relationships, where each side knows the other will stand firm when needed. However, building such closeness may take time. Scorpio does not open up right away, testing potential friends or partners to confirm sincerity. Meanwhile, if someone close breaks trust, the hurt can run deep. Repair is possible if the one at fault shows real regret and changed behavior, but Scorpio is cautious about repeating mistakes. Over the years, they refine who they trust, often ending up with a close circle of dependable people.

Scorpios often show quiet leadership skills. While they may not seek to be the loudest voice in a room, they can guide teams by noticing unspoken problems or by suggesting well-researched solutions. This approach can be powerful, as they prefer to act based on facts and thorough understanding. Their calm under pressure helps in crises—others might panic, but Scorpio remains steady, analyzing the situation. Some colleagues appreciate this calm approach, while a few might mistakenly see it as aloofness. Once people recognize Scorpio's commitment to fairness and results, they often rely on them for guidance in complex or demanding tasks.

In family life, Scorpio can be protective, sometimes to an extreme. They want to shield loved ones from harm or dishonesty. If a sibling or child is bullied, Scorpio may step in decisively. If a relative is ill or worried, Scorpio might gather resources and solutions. Balancing this protective side is essential, since family members need room to solve their own problems, too. By learning to help without controlling, Scorpio fosters healthy bonds. They can become the relative that others call when serious advice or comfort is needed. Their emotional insight, combined with a sense of responsibility, makes them a dependable anchor for the family.

In love or deeper relationships, Scorpio's devotion can be a gift. Partners may feel secure, knowing that Scorpio invests wholeheartedly once trust is established. Emotional intensity can spice up romance, but it can also bring drama if jealousy or suspicion flares. Clear communication helps both sides handle disagreements smoothly. Scorpio's partner must understand that privacy is part of Scorpio's nature, not a sign of disinterest. Meanwhile, Scorpio can remember that healthy partners deserve a window into their inner world now and then. When balanced, Scorpio's relationships are marked by warmth, steadiness, and an unspoken bond that weaves two lives closely together.

Regarding career, Scorpios often do well in positions that tap into their investigative mind. They might be drawn to fields like science, research, criminal justice, psychology, finance, or technology. Their patience and detail-oriented style can unearth overlooked information. If they run a business, they carefully plan finances and strategies, sometimes surprising competitors who expected a more showy approach. Challenges arise if a workplace has unclear ethics or fosters gossip. Scorpios prefer a work culture that respects honesty and depth. When they find a suitable environment, they tend to stay loyal, quietly rising through the ranks or honing specialized skills that make them indispensable.

Scorpios also display creativity, though it might show up in less obvious ways. Some write poetry or stories with emotional punch. Others craft or paint, placing hidden symbolism in their art. Even outside traditional "art," a Scorpio might apply creativity in coding, problem-solving, or designing unique solutions at work. They might not always show their creative side to everyone, choosing to keep personal projects for themselves or a select group. Still, many enjoy channeling their deep feelings into artistic pursuits. Doing so helps them process life experiences and maintain balance. Over time, these quiet creative efforts can blossom into remarkable expressions of the Scorpio spirit.

Scorpio's teenage years and early adulthood often set the stage for how they will handle relationships and challenges later. During that time, they may learn lessons about trusting the wrong person or holding onto grudges too tightly. Mistakes can happen, but they often guide a Scorpio toward wiser approaches. If they keep an open mind, these early experiences can sharpen their intuition for identifying genuine friends or safe opportunities. By the time they reach midlife, they may have a stronger sense of self, using prior missteps as fuel for improvement. In old age, they can become a source of wisdom for younger kin and community members.

An important aspect is acknowledging that Scorpios are not all the same. Their rising signs, moon signs, personal backgrounds, and life events also influence how they behave. Some Scorpios are more outgoing, some are more introverted. Some embrace calm hobbies, others thrive on physical challenges or adventurous travel. The common thread tends to be emotional commitment and a longing for truth in whatever they do. People might meet multiple Scorpios in their life, noticing that each expresses these qualities differently. Whether it is a calm teacher or a dynamic coworker, the Scorpio spark is there—displayed in loyalty, thoroughness, or a soulful approach to tasks.

Many myths paint Scorpio as either dangerous or magical, but reality is more nuanced. By seeing how Scorpios handle everyday affairs—friendships, problem-solving, personal growth—one understands they are human, just with a notable inclination for depth. While some might cling to negativity, most learn to use their strong will in helpful ways. The sign's symbol, the scorpion, reminds us of self-protection and hidden power. Yet the scorpion only stings when threatened; it spends much time quietly minding its own survival. In similar fashion, a balanced Scorpio typically seeks peace and fairness, but stands prepared to defend what matters if threats arise.

Scorpio's link to transformation appears in astrology, often associated with the idea of rising from hardships stronger than before. This can be seen when a Scorpio faces a major setback—loss of a job, the end of a relationship, or a personal crisis. Though they might brood initially, many turn that pain into motivation for growth. They reorganize their priorities, remove toxic influences, and improve themselves. Outsiders sometimes marvel at how a Scorpio can go through tough times but emerge with renewed focus or a new skill. This pattern fits the idea of turning adversity into a chance for self-improvement, a core theme in Scorpio's astrological tradition.

In family structures, Scorpio children can display maturity beyond their years, quietly observing adult conversations or household routines. As siblings, they might protect younger brothers or sisters fiercely, or keep a watchful eye on older ones. Parents raising them should balance respecting privacy with ensuring open communication. In turn, Scorpio parents teach children values like trust, honesty, and perseverance. The key is to avoid making things too rigid or secretive at home. Openness about feelings can foster a healthy emotional climate, preventing the child from feeling the need to hide every thought. This results in a stable family environment where children feel safe expressing themselves.

As friends, Scorpios often bring sincerity to a group, even if they are not the most vocal. They listen closely to personal stories and might offer advice that shows they have weighed each angle. Friends learn that if they confide in a Scorpio, the information is likely kept private. That sense of confidentiality fosters trust. If a friend is in trouble, Scorpio can quietly rally support or resources. But Scorpios also expect loyalty in return—when they do not get it, disappointment hits hard. A Scorpio friend might disappear from a social circle if they feel repeatedly let down. Building or mending trust in friendship requires mutual respect and consistent actions.

At work, Scorpio's presence can foster a culture of careful planning and thorough follow-through. If they spot inefficiencies, they might approach management with a well-researched proposal. Their suggestions often carry weight because they have analyzed potential flaws. However, Scorpios may need to share ideas earlier in the process to let teammates offer input. This teamwork can create even stronger outcomes. If the workplace is filled with gossip or unclear goals, Scorpio might retreat. They do not see value in shallow interactions. In a more respectful environment, they can thrive, using their steady effort to boost group results. Over time, they become known for reliability and calm effectiveness.

On an emotional level, Scorpio's introspection can help them move through personal transformations. They might reflect deeply at certain milestones—like turning a significant age or shifting careers—asking, "Am I on the right track?" If they find something lacking, they do not fear tearing down old structures to build something new. Yet they do this carefully, not in a hasty manner. Others might view them as fearless, but it is more about being thorough and courageous when faced with big changes. As they grow older, many Scorpios learn to handle these personal changes with less drama, focusing on steady steps that align with their long-term values.

When it comes to spiritual or philosophical questions, Scorpios often show curiosity about life's mysteries. They could explore different traditions, read about deeper concepts, or test various meditative practices to see what resonates. Some might find meaning in quietly supporting others, believing that small, genuine acts reflect a deeper purpose. Others might join study groups that discuss moral or metaphysical topics. Regardless of the path, a Scorpio typically wants sincerity and not just surface gestures. They want experiences or beliefs that stand up to scrutiny. This reflective nature helps them form a sense of inner security, even if they keep many spiritual thoughts private.

In relationships with other signs, Scorpio's success hinges on mutual respect and acceptance of differences. If they pair with a lively fire sign, they can discover new adventures, provided both compromise on how fast to move and how much to reveal. If they team up with an earth sign, they might form stable routines and shared goals. Air signs can open Scorpio's mind to broader perspectives, though Scorpio must adapt to the air sign's lighter style. Water signs share emotional language, but they must avoid drowning in each other's feelings. Each combination can work if they recognize that their distinct methods can complement rather than clash.

In summary, Scorpio's life is shaped by themes of emotional depth, trust, protective instincts, and a thoughtful approach to tasks. While the scorpion symbol can suggest danger or secrecy, a balanced Scorpio uses these qualities to maintain healthy relationships, excel in chosen fields, and remain loyal to the people who matter most. Myths may claim Scorpios are purely vengeful or controlling, but reality shows they can be supportive, caring, and highly dependable when bonds are honest. For Scorpio and those around them, understanding this sign's strengths and potential pitfalls can build bridges of respect. By sharing insights, we allow Scorpio's positive traits—like tenacity, loyalty, and focus—to flourish, benefiting not just the Scorpio individual but the communities they are part of.

If you are a Scorpio, remember that your way of seeing the world is valuable. Your attention to detail and emotional insight can help solve problems that require thorough understanding. Your loyalty can nurture relationships that last for years. At the same time, be kind to yourself about any mistakes. No one is perfect, and your sign does not require you to be flawless. If you are a friend, partner, or coworker of a Scorpio, respect their need for privacy and avoid pressuring them to share everything at once. Show sincerity, and you will likely find a companion or colleague who stands by you.

Looking back at the entire picture, Scorpio represents depth in many forms—whether in personal reflection, loyalty to friends, or committed pursuit of goals. The sign highlights how strong emotions, when channeled properly, can produce growth and resilience. Scorpio's interest in discovering hidden truths can reveal bigger lessons about trust, honesty, and personal responsibility. By seeing how this sign appears in various areas of life—childhood, adulthood, social connections, work, and beyond—we realize that each Scorpio has a chance to shape their path with courage and empathy. These final thoughts encourage both Scorpios and non-Scorpios to appreciate the sign's essence while honoring individuality.

Scorpio's story is one of transformation, reflective thought, and profound caring. If you relate strongly to Scorpio traits, you may have noticed recurring patterns—like a tendency to read emotions well or a preference for building a few deep friendships rather than many casual ones. There is power in recognizing these patterns. You can harness them for personal growth, searching for friendships or careers that let your honesty and determination shine. Additionally, you can handle the potential downsides—like distrust or grudges—by employing methods that encourage open dialogue and self-forgiveness. This two-sided understanding can unlock a balanced, fulfilling life journey guided by integrity.

In many ways, the entire discussion of Scorpio points to a sign that craves purpose. Whether it is investigating a mystery, caring for a loved one, or staying late at work to finish a critical task, Scorpios want actions that hold real meaning. This can push them to excel in jobs that involve helping others, digging into research, or building something that lasts. It can also drive them to form relationships that stand the test of time, as they put heart and soul into these connections. When they see that their energy is serving a higher cause or forging a lasting bond, they feel truly motivated.

As we close these chapters, one last note is the value of acceptance—for Scorpios to accept themselves and for others to accept Scorpio's unique approach. Self-acceptance means recognizing that your preference for quieter gatherings or deeper topics does not make you antisocial. It is part of who you are. Acceptance from others means they see your caution or need for privacy not as coldness, but as a sign that you take trust seriously. Together, these forms of understanding create a more harmonious environment. Scorpios then feel confident to share their loyalty, emotional insight, and solutions, enriching any group or relationship they join.

Whether you are a Scorpio or just have a Scorpio friend or colleague, keep in mind that learning about zodiac traits is only one part of truly knowing someone. Life experiences, personal choices, and cultural background shape each person in ways that may confirm or twist typical zodiac patterns. Still, by looking at Scorpio's common features—deep feelings, strong resolve, cautious trust—we gain hints about how to connect productively. We see that giving them time to open up, honoring their devotion, and respecting their boundaries can yield stable, authentic relationships. Scorpios themselves can harness these insights for self-growth, forging a path that uses both heart and mind.

If you are inspired to learn more, you might want to explore your entire birth chart or read further about astrological traditions. Just remember that signs are a starting point, not a final label. Focus on daily habits, moral values, and how you handle adversity, because these real-life behaviors define you beyond your sun sign. For Scorpios, continuing to refine communication skills, staying flexible in the face of change, and remembering to celebrate progress can lead to a more content and impactful life. Likewise, friends and family of a Scorpio can keep building trust by offering consistent respect and honesty.

As new chapters unfold in a Scorpio's life, they might continue to refine the lessons we have discussed: open yet respectful communication, balanced emotional expression, and fair handling of power dynamics. For some Scorpios, the next big step could be shifting careers or learning new personal skills, all approached with trademark focus. For others, it might mean deepening family ties or exploring volunteer roles. The sign's capacity for depth ensures that whatever they do, they do it wholeheartedly. This sense of commitment often turns ordinary tasks into experiences filled with meaning, leaving a strong impression on those around them.

In the grand view of astrology, Scorpio stands among the twelve signs as a symbol of intensity, loyalty, and the power of transformation. While certain stereotypes claim it is all about revenge or secrecy, a more balanced perspective reveals that a healthy Scorpio uses determination for good causes and keeps private matters safe rather than hidden for sinister reasons. As we have explored, Scorpios can be warm and generous once trust is formed. They can excel in teamwork if they learn to share insights promptly. Above all, they aim to remain genuine in an often confusing world—a mission that resonates with people from all signs.

Our deep dive into Scorpio's essence highlights that each sign has lessons to offer. From Scorpio, we can learn the importance of commitment, the strength in cautious trust, and the wonder of deeper connections. Scorpio's path is not about being perfect or controlling everyone's secrets; it is about finding harmony in life's hidden corners, protecting loved ones with sincerity, and standing firm on one's values. As you step away from these chapters, consider how Scorpio's example might inspire you—whether you share this sign or not. Perhaps there is a skill you can pursue with more focus, or a relationship you can strengthen through honest communication.

To all Scorpios reading: keep exploring your inner depths and remember that caring for yourself is part of caring for others. Let your curiosity, empathy, and determination guide you to new experiences that spark your growth. Do not shy away from challenges, but ensure you have balance in rest and enjoyment, too. For those with Scorpio friends or loved ones, appreciate the steadfast loyalty they bring. Understand their boundaries, respect their trust, and you will find a companion capable of offering firm support. Together, these mutual efforts enrich friendships, families, workplaces, and communities in ways that reflect the best of Scorpio's spirit.

In essence, Scorpio stands for the idea that true strength arises from honest self-knowledge and a commitment to meaningful bonds. This sign reminds us that unwavering focus, emotional bravery, and the courage to transform challenges into growth can shape a fulfilling life. Whether dealing with heartbreak or celebrating a milestone quietly, Scorpios approach moments with depth and sincerity. By balancing self-protection with openness, they can forge paths marked by loyalty and understanding. May these final reflections serve as a reminder that while each Scorpio's journey is unique, their shared qualities can light a path toward rewarding personal success and steadfast connections.

We have traveled through all the different aspects of Scorpio—its history, myths, daily life, emotions, and connections to others. These chapters show that beneath the mysterious image lies a sign built on substance and care. Scorpios, at their core, want to stay true to what they believe in and secure strong, genuine bonds with those around them. Through learning to manage strong feelings well, communicate openly, and share their gifts, they can shape an environment where trust and truth flourish. This is the real power of Scorpio: not stinging foes, but nurturing a life guided by genuine commitments and thoughtful understanding.

Thank you for reading about Scorpio. If you are a Scorpio yourself, remember the tips and ideas here are meant to encourage your strengths and guide you past common roadblocks. If you have Scorpios in your life, hopefully you feel more prepared to appreciate their quiet resilience and empathize with the challenges they face. Each sign has wisdom to offer, and Scorpio's gift is teaching us the importance of honesty, loyalty, and depth. By blending these qualities with kindness, whether at home or in the outside world, Scorpios can leave a lasting positive mark. May this book be a resource for better understanding and closer connections.

Help Us Share Your Thoughts!

Dear reader,

Thank you for spending your time with this book. We hope it brought you enjoyment and a few new ideas to think about. If there was anything that didn't work for you, or if you have suggestions on how we can improve, please let us know at **kontakt@skriuwer.com**. Your feedback means a lot to us and helps us make our books even better.

If you enjoyed this book, we would be very grateful if you left a review on the site where you purchased it. Your review not only helps other readers find our books, but also encourages us to keep creating more stories and materials that you'll love.

By choosing Skriuwer, you're also supporting **Frisian**—a minority language mainly spoken in the northern Netherlands. Although **Frisian** has a rich history, the number of speakers is shrinking, and it's at risk of dying out. Your purchase helps fund resources to preserve and promote this language, such as educational programs and learning tools. If you'd like to learn more about Frisian or even start learning it yourself, please visit **www.learnfrisian.com**.

Thank you for being part of our community. We look forward to sharing more books with you in the future.

Warm regards,
The Skriuwer Team

www.ingramcontent.com/pod-product-compliance
Lightning Source LLC
LaVergne TN
LVHW012044070526
838202LV00056B/5587